LAW, CRIME AND LAW ENFORCEMENT

ORGANIZED RETAIL CRIME

12714

LAW, CRIME AND LAW ENFORCEMENT

Additional books in this series can be found on Nova's website under the Series tab.

Additional E-books in this series can be found on Nova's website under the E-books tab.

LAW, CRIME AND LAW ENFORCEMENT

Nova Science Publishers, Inc.
New York

LIBRARY OF CONGRESS CATALOGING-IN-PUBLICATION DATA

Organized retail crime / Editors: Blake H. Liventin.
p. cm.
Includes index.
ISBN 978-1-61122-768-0 (softcover)
1. Shoplifting--United States. 2. Organized crime--United States. 3. Retail trade--Security measures--United States. I. Liventin, Blake H. II. United States. Congress. House. Committee on the Judiciary. Subcommittee on Crime, Terrorism, and Homeland Security.
KF9352.A25 2010
345.73'026232--dc22
2010043943

Published by Nova Science Publishers, Inc. † New York

CONTENTS

PREFACE

Organized retail crime (ORC), also known as organized retail theft, typically refers to large-scale retail theft and fraud by organized groups of professional shoplifters or "boosters." The organized crime rings resell this illegally acquired merchandise via a variety of "fencing" operations such as flea markets, swap meets, pawn shops, and online marketplaces. These goods are sold to both individual buyers as well as retailers. This book provides an overview of organized retail crime rings, their operations, and goods targeted, and examines the domestic impact of ORC in the arenas of the economy, public health and safety, and domestic security. This book also outlines current efforts by retailers, resale markets and the federal government to combat ORC.

Chapter 1- Organized retail crime (ORC) involves the large-scale theft of everyday consumer items and potentially has much broader implications. Organized groups of professional shoplifters, or "boosters," steal or fraudulently obtain merchandise that is then sold, or "fenced," to individuals and retailers through a variety of venues. In an increasingly globalized society, more and more transactions take place online rather than face-to-face. As such, in addition to relying on physical resale markets, organized retail thieves have turned to online marketplaces as means to fence their ill-gotten goods.

Chapter 2- What is called Organized Retail Theft or ORT by Retail Loss Prevention Professionals, can generally be described as professional burglars, boosters, cons, thieves, fences and resellers conspiring to steal and sell retail merchandise obtained from retail establishments by theft or deception. 'Boosters' – the front line thieves who intend to resell stolen goods – generally coordinate with 'fences' who may sell the items outright at flea markets or convenience stores or online; or repackage them for sale to higher level fences. The problem is significant for its negative economic impact, the safety issues it brings to unsuspecting consumers, and its potential link to other criminal enterprises.

Chapter 3- , I would like to thank you for the opportunity to testify today on the efforts of U.S. Immigration and Customs Enforcement (ICE) in the area of Organized Retail Crime (ORC). As you know, ICE is the largest investigative agency within the Department of Homeland Security. We protect national security and uphold public safety by targeting transnational criminal networks and terrorist organizations that seek to exploit vulnerabilities at our borders.

Chapter 4- While the Secret Service is perhaps best known for protecting our nation's leaders, we were established in 1865 to investigate and prevent the counterfeiting of United States currency. As the original guardian of the nation's financial payment system, the Secret Service has a long history of protecting American consumers, industries, and financial institutions from fraud. Congress continues to recognize the Secret Service's 144 years of investigative expertise in financial crimes and over the last two decades has expanded our statutory authorities to include access device fraud (18 USC §1029), which includes credit and debit card fraud. Congress has also given the Secret Service concurrent jurisdiction with other law enforcement agencies for identity theft (18 USC §1028), computer fraud (18 USC §1030), and bank fraud (18 USC §1344). We take our mission to combat these crimes seriously and as a result, the Secret Service is recognized worldwide for its investigative expertise and innovative approaches to detecting, investigating, and preventing financial crimes.

Chapter 5- The Postal Inspection Service has a long, proud, and successful history of securing the nation's mail system and ensuring the public's trust in the mail. Postal Inspectors have been fighting consumer fraud since the mail fraud statute was enacted in 1872. The company name, address and "product" may change, but con artists take advantage of economic trends and current events to plan their schemes and illegal activities. With modern technology, the potential for the American public to be defrauded through the mail is much greater and potentially impacts more people than ever before.

Chapter 6- By way of background, the Coalition Against Organized Retail Crime, which has been together now for six years, is comprised of national manufacturing and retail organizations as well as individual companies from both sectors. In total, there are 32 members. A roster of all Coalition members can be found at the end of this written testimony. We are also pleased to recognize the formal support of the International Association of Chiefs of

Police (IACP) in our effort to control retail crime and the Internet fencing of stolen property.

Chapter 7- Prior to joining eBay in 1999, I was an Assistant United States Attorney in the Eastern District of Virginia for 11 years. For 5 of those years I served as Chief of the Major Crimes Unit. My career at eBay has been focused on keeping our site safe for our community by working with the law enforcement community, the private sector, policymakers, consumer protection agencies and state and federal legislatures, so I very much appreciate the opportunity to speak with you today on behalf of eBay about this important topic.

Chapter 8- I have been invited here to share with you our experience with the increasing problem of organized retail crime (ORC). Retailers have always had to deal with shoplifting as part of doing business, but let me be clear, ORC is not shoplifting. It is theft committed by professionals, in large volume, for resale. It is being committed against retailers of every type at an increasing rate. Safeway estimates a loss of $100 million dollars annually due to ORC. According to the FBI, the national estimate is between $15-30 billion annually.

Chapter 9- By way of background, I am currently a detective with the Montgomery County Police Department's Retail Crimes Unit and have been in law enforcement for over 16 years. I am a sworn Deputy of the U.S. Marshall Service and assigned to the Metro Area Fraud Task Force of the United States Secret Service. I am the *only* detective in my department and one of the few in the region assigned exclusively to investigate retail theft and fraud.

In: Organized Retail Crime
Editors: Blake H. Liventin

ISBN: 978-1-61122-768-0

Chapter 1

ORGANIZED RETAIL CRIME

Kristin M. Finklea

SUMMARY

Organized retail crime (ORC) involves the large-scale theft of everyday consumer items and potentially has much broader implications. Organized groups of professional shoplifters, or "boosters," steal or fraudulently obtain merchandise that is then sold, or "fenced," to individuals and retailers through a variety of venues. In an increasingly globalized society, more and more transactions take place online rather than face-to-face. As such, in addition to relying on physical resale markets, organized retail thieves have turned to online marketplaces as means to fence their ill-gotten goods.

ORC exposes the United States to costs and harms in the economic, public health, and domestic security arenas. The exact loss from ORC to the retail industry is unknown, but an often-cited estimate of this loss is $15 billion to $30 billion annually. The economic impact, however, extends beyond the manufacturing and retail industry and includes costs incurred by consumers and taxes lost by the states. The theft and resale of stolen consumable or health and beauty products such as infant formula (that may have been repackaged, relabeled, and subjected to altered expiration dates) poses potential safety concerns for individuals purchasing such goods from ORC fences. In addition, some industry experts and policy makers have expressed concern about the possibility that proceeds from ORC may be used to fund terrorist activities.

Current efforts to combat ORC largely come from retailers, online marketplaces, and law enforcement alike. Retailers responding to the 2008 National Retail Security Survey spent an average of 0.34% of their annual sales on loss prevention measures. These loss prevention costs are ultimately born by the consumers in the form of higher prices on goods. Also, online marketplaces report taking various measures to combat the sale of stolen and fraudulently obtained goods on their websites, including educating sellers and consumers, monitoring suspicious activity, and partnering with retailers and law enforcement. Combating retail theft has traditionally been handled by state law enforcement under state criminal laws. Some, however, have begun to question whether state laws—which vary in the quantity of monetary losses that constitute major theft—are adequate to combat ORC.

While many agree that ORC is a national problem, there is debate over the federal government's role in deterring ORC and sanctioning various actors that may be involved in committing or aiding these crimes. One policy issue facing Congress is whether criminalizing organized retail crime in the *U.S. Code* would allow for more effective investigation and prosecution of these criminals. Congress may also wish to consider whether regulating resale marketplaces (online markets, in particular), to require such entities to increase information sharing with retailers and law enforcement, would strengthen investigations and prosecutions of ORC as well as decrease the prevalence of retail thieves relying on legitimate online marketplaces to fence stolen goods. Several pieces of legislation have been introduced in the 111th Congress that would address these issues.

INTRODUCTION

Organized retail crime (ORC), often referred to as organized retail theft, typically refers to large-scale retail theft and fraud by organized groups of professional shoplifters, or "boosters."[1] It is an umbrella term encompassing a variety of retail crimes, including theft, gift card fraud, receipt fraud, ticket switching,[2] and cargo theft, just to name a few. Stolen and fraudulently obtained goods may be taken not only from retailers, but from manufacturers and distributors as well. The organized crime rings resell this illegally acquired merchandise via a variety of "fencing" operations such as flea markets, swap meets, pawn shops, and online marketplaces; these goods are sold to both individual buyers as well as retailers—potentially the very retailers from where the merchandise was originally stolen. ORC differs fundamentally from shoplifting in that amateur shoplifters tend to steal merchandise for personal consumption. Boosters, on the other hand, are professional thieves who make money by stealing merchandise from retail and other venues and reselling it to fences who in turn sell the goods—through legal or illegal economic outlets—for a fraction of the retail cost.

Organized retail crime exposes the United States to economic, public health, and domestic security dangers. It is a national problem, not only for retailers, but for manufacturers, consumers, taxpayers, and the states as well. According to one industry survey, about 90% of retailers surveyed in 2010 reported having been victimized by ORC in the previous 12 months. This is a decrease from the 92% that reported victimization in 2009 but still greater than the 85% that reported victimization in 2008.[3] Estimates of retail losses to ORC range from as low as $15 billion to as high as $37 billion annually.[4] And this is the loss to retailers alone. The monetary loss, however, extends beyond the retail industry to the taxpayers and states. Consumers pay for these losses in the form of higher prices on goods, and states lose the tax revenue that would otherwise be generated from the sale of these goods by legitimate retailers.

In addition to the economic impact of ORC, the theft and resale of stolen consumable or health and beauty products, such as infant formula, may pose safety risks to individuals purchasing such goods from ORC fences. This is because such products may have been repackaged, relabeled, subjected to altered expiration dates, or stored improperly before being reentered into commerce. In addition, industry experts, law enforcement, and policy makers have expressed concern about the possibility that proceeds from ORC may be used to fund terrorist activities.[5] In particular, federal law enforcement has reputedly traced the illicit proceeds from the theft and resale of infant formula to terrorist organizations and insurgent groups, including Hamas and Hezbollah.[6]

Combating retail theft has traditionally been handled by state law enforcement under state criminal laws.[7] Some, however, have begun to question whether state laws—which vary in the quantity of monetary losses that constitute major theft[8]—are adequate to combat ORC. While many agree that ORC is a national problem, there is debate over the federal government's role in deterring ORC and sanctioning various actors that may be involved in committing or aiding these crimes. One policy issue facing Congress is whether criminalizing organized retail crime in the *U.S. Code* would allow for more effective investigation and prosecution of these criminals. Another related issue that Congress may wish to consider is whether regulating resale marketplaces (online markets, in particular), to require such entities to increase information sharing with retailers and law enforcement, would strengthen investigations and prosecutions of ORC as well as decrease the prevalence of retail thieves relying on legitimate online marketplaces to fence stolen goods.

This chapter provides an overview of organized retail crime rings, their operations, and goods targeted. It then examines the domestic impact of ORC in the arenas of the economy, public health and safety, and domestic security. The report also outlines current efforts by retailers, resale markets, and the federal government to combat ORC. It then analyzes various policy issues that the 111th Congress may wish to consider, including whether current federal resources provided for the investigation of ORC are adequate, whether to amend the *U.S. Code* to criminalize ORC, and whether to regulate resale marketplaces that may be utilized as fences for criminals to sell stolen goods.

Challenges in Defining of Organized Retail Crime

The concept of organized retail crime tends to be discussed in terms of criminal networks engaged in large-scale theft. Descriptions of ORC also generally entail criminals fraudulently obtaining goods in quantities beyond what would normally be intended for personal consumption; reselling these ill-gotten goods; receiving, concealing, transporting, or disposing of these goods; or coordinating individuals to commit these retail crimes.[9] There is a lack of consensus, however, on the specific activities—particularly of boosters—that constitute ORC. On the one hand, most agree that ORC involves store theft or fraud schemes designed to obtain retail merchandise at a cost significantly below retail value or for free. However, some also include specific activities, such as cargo theft,[10] in the definition of ORC,[11] while others either omit certain activities or do not specify the range of ORC activities.[12] For example, federal law enforcement agencies, such as the Federal Bureau of Investigation (FBI), tend to constrain discussions of ORC to situations in which boosters steal merchandise from retail establishments and resell it for profit. Similarly, retail organizations have generally focused on store theft when describing the problem of ORC. One possible explanation for this focus on store theft is that, although ORC may encompass multiple activities, including store theft and cargo theft, store theft has been cited as the most common.[13] Because retail organizations, scholars, industry experts, and law enforcement have provided varying definitions of ORC, this complicates analysts' abilities to evaluate the exact impact of ORC.[14]

Federal Definition

Currently, ORC is not a federal crime. Issues surrounding the debate over whether it should be included in the federal criminal code are analyzed later in this chapter. For data collection purposes, however, Congress has defined ORC as

- violating a state ban against shoplifting or retail merchandise theft—if the quantities of items stolen are of the amount that would not normally be purchased for personal use or consumption—and stealing for the purposes of reselling the items or reentering them into commerce;
- receiving, possessing, concealing, bartering, selling, transporting, or disposing of any property that is known to have been taken in the violation outlined above; or
- coordinating, organizing, or recruiting persons to undertake either of the two violations outlined above.[15]

Operation of Organized Retail Crime Groups

As mentioned, organized retail crime rings generally include individuals serving in one of two main capacities: boosters or fences. Generally, boosters act as professional shoplifters who steal or illegally obtain merchandise. Fences pay boosters for stolen goods and then resell them to witting or unwitting consumers and businesses.

Boosters work either alone or in groups to steal goods that they will later sell to fences for about 10% to 25% of the ticket value.[16] They often carry "fence sheets," or shopping lists provided to boosters by fences. These shopping lists itemize the goods fences desire, the amounts fences will pay for each item, and retail store locations where each item may be.[17] In some cases, boosters may travel across state lines to target specific establishments in multiple states. Consequently, many boosters will at some point transport stolen merchandise across state lines, either when shipping stolen goods to a fence or when physically delivering merchandise to a fence after stealing it in another state.

Fencing operations can be very straightforward or can involve multiple stages and a degree of operational sophistication. Most stolen merchandise is sold to a low-level fence, commonly called a "street fence." Street fences will either sell these goods directly to the public—through flea markets, swap meets, or the Internet—or will sell the merchandise to mid-level fences who run "cleaning operations." Cleaning operations remove security tags and store labels as well as repackage stolen goods so they appear as though they came directly from the manufacturer. A notable concern for public health and safety, this cleaning process may even involve changing the expiration date on perishable goods.[18] The "clean" goods may then be sold to the public or to higher-level fences, who often operate illegitimate wholesale businesses. Through these businesses, the fences can supply merchandise to retailers, often mixing stolen merchandise with legitimate goods. The illegal activities of fences may be of concern for policy makers and federal law enforcement because—like boosters—fences' activities may cross state lines. They may, for instance, purchase stolen goods from boosters in one state and send them to another state to be cleaned; they may then sell this "clean" merchandise to illegitimate wholesalers in another state. In addition, fences selling goods via online marketplaces may ship stolen goods across state or national lines.

Targeted Products

Investigations of organized retail crime rings have uncovered a wide variety of goods targeted to be stolen and resold on the black market. One researcher has noted that CRAVED items (meaning those goods that are Concealable, Removable, Available, Valuable, Enjoyable, and Disposable) are more often targeted because of the ease with which criminals can remove these items from stores and convert them into cash or other valuables.[19] On the one hand, some desirable—or "hot"[20]—products, such as cigarettes and alcohol, may always be popular products for thieves. The desirability of other products may be based on their current popularity (such as new movies, video games, and music titles) or on their use in drug manufacturing activities (such as ephedrine-based cold medications and lithium batteries). In addition, the popularity of products may also be brand-specific. For example, while certain brands of razor blades, printer cartridges, and designer clothing may be frequently targeted for theft, competing brands may be ignored.[21] Current desirable items, in no specific order, include

- tobacco products;
- premium razor blades;
- face creams;
- analgesics;
- smoking cessation products;
- designer, logo, and leather apparel and shoes (particularly athletic);
- name-brand power tools;
- vacuum cleaners;
- printer ink cartridges;
- steaks;
- film;
- coffee;
- consumer electronics (such as DVD players and GPS units);
- fragrances;
- infant formula;
- batteries;
  music and game DVDs; and
- over-the-counter (OTC) medications and test kits.[22]

Methods Used by Boosters

Boosters working in groups rather than alone often have at least one member of the group act as a lookout who scouts for employees, plain clothes security officers, or cameras. These lookouts may create diversions or distract employees to facilitate the work of the boosters actually stealing the merchandise.[23]

To help prevent thieves from stealing these goods, many retailers place electronic detection tags on merchandise. Boosters often circumvent detection systems by cutting off or melting the tags, covering the tags in foil or concealing the merchandise in foil-lined bags (often referred to as "magic" bags), or lifting goods over the antennas of the electronic detection systems.[24] In some instances, boosters take shopping bags directly from the store, fill them with merchandise, and walk out of the store, appearing as though they are carrying purchased goods. Store employees may be less likely to stop and question boosters carrying shopping bags from the store because they incorrectly assume that the merchandise has indeed been paid for.[25]

In addition, boosters do not always steal merchandise from retailers during business hours. Some may hide in stores and wait for all employees to leave before removing large amounts of goods through emergency exits. Others conduct "smash-and-grab" burglaries, in which they steal trucks and vans to ram through store walls and windows, load the vehicles with merchandise, and drive away.[26]

Employee Collusion

At times, boosters also conspire with current or former store employees. Employees may take goods from storage rooms or receiving areas in stores and provide them directly to boosters. They may also help thieves by disabling store alarms, leaving doors unlocked, or providing information about computer passwords, alarm codes, keys, and management and security schedules.[27] Industry studies estimated the proportion of inventory loss due to employee theft.[28] However, it is currently unknown how often employee theft or fraud is directly implicated in cases of organized retail crime. For example, the 2008 National Retail Security Survey reports that retailers estimate about 42.7% of retail losses are due to employee theft. They further estimate that about 14.4% of these internal losses involve employees colluding with individuals outside of the given retail store. Of this 14.4% of internal loss cases, an unknown proportion may be attributed to employees working with organized retail criminals.[29]

Fraud Schemes

Not all organized retail crime involves traditional theft from retail stores. ORC groups have employed numerous tactics to defraud retailers and obtain merchandise. Take, for instance, receipt fraud. In these cases, thieves steal merchandise, create counterfeit receipts for the stolen goods, return these stolen goods to the retailers using the counterfeit receipts, and collect money off of the fraudulent returns.[30] This cuts out the fence altogether, potentially netting a higher return.

Another method by which ORC groups defraud retailers is through gift card fraud, of which there are several forms. For one, thieves may purchase legitimate gift cards using stolen credit cards and then sell the gift cards to the highest bidder using an online auction website. In other instances, thieves may purchase low-value gift cards, electronically reprogram the cards to contain a higher value, and resell these reprogrammed cards.[31]

Similarly, ORC thieves may use ticket-switching scams to fraudulently obtain high-value items at a relatively low cost. Thieves use devices that create fake barcodes that they adhere to packages, covering the original barcodes; when scanned, these new barcodes ring up the items at lower costs. If, at check-out, a retail employee scanning the barcodes is not paying close attention or does not have a strong knowledge of items' values, the thief may get away with paying the price indicated by the counterfeit barcode. Criminals can then resell, or fence, the goods at prices higher than those which they paid, but still lower than their retail values.[32]

Cargo Theft

As mentioned, some scholars and experts include cargo theft as an element of organized retail crime while others do not. It is nonetheless of value to note how retail goods are vulnerable to criminals at various points throughout the supply chain. Further, goods that are stolen from either cargo trucks or from retail stores may be fenced by criminals for a profit, and both affect society's economy, public health, and domestic security.

Because trains and trucks of cargo often travel with large quantities of desirable products, some have suggested that this presents a low-risk, high-reward situation appealing to criminals.[33] Thieves use a variety of methods to obtain merchandise from cargo, from hijacking entire trucks to colluding with current or former employees. These criminals may break or compromise security locks on trucks (possibly with the aid of security codes provided by dishonest employees) to remove entire boxes of desired goods. Other times, they may pilfer cargo boxes of their goods and then reseal them so the boxes appear as though they have not been tampered with.[34]

Methods Used by Fences

Fences use various methods to sell stolen goods that they purchase from boosters. As mentioned, some fences may sell stolen merchandise back to retailers through illegitimate wholesale operations. They may also operate legitimate business, such as pawn shops, convenience stores, repair shops, second-hand stores, and salvage yards, that serve as fronts for their illegal fencing operations.[35] In addition, fences may sell their goods at a variety of resale marketplaces, including flea markets. At flea markets, illegitimate wholesalers are able to sell stolen goods that have been damaged and cannot be resold to retailers. Also, flea markets have been known to serve as recruiting grounds for fences looking for boosters, and vice-versa.[36]

Impact of Globalization and Technology

In an increasingly globalized society, more and more transactions take place online rather than face-to-face. As such, in addition to relying on physical resale markets, organized retail thieves have turned to the Internet and online marketplaces as means to fence their ill-gotten goods.[37] This practice of fencing via the Internet is commonly referred to as "e-fencing." According to the most recent National Retail Federation survey of retailers, about 66% of surveyed retailers indicated that they had identified or recovered stolen merchandise (including gift cards) that was being fenced online.[38] Further, over one-quarter of the retailers indicated that more than half of the "new in box" items sold on auction websites may be stolen or fraudulently obtained.[39]

E-fencing has affected organized retail crime in several arenas, including criminal anonymity, global reach, and profitability. Whereas criminals fencing goods at physical locations (such as flea markets) must have face-to-face interactions, those who rely on e-fencing are better able to remain anonymous to customers, victimized retailers, and law enforcement alike. Further, the use of online markets has allowed criminals to more easily distribute stolen goods not only within the metropolitan areas where they were originally obtained, but throughout the United States and across the globe. E-fencing has also proven to be more profitable to criminals than has fencing at physical locations; while criminals may profit about 30 cents on the dollar (30% of the retail price) by selling goods at physical fencing locations, they can make about 70 cents on the dollar via e-fencing.[40] It has been suggested that the face-to-face nature of physical marketplaces allows consumers to recognize the questionable legality of goods, and thus consumers are willing to pay less for goods in these physical markets than online.[41]

DOMESTIC IMPACT OF ORGANIZED RETAIL CRIME

At first glance, the impact of organized retail crime may appear to be limited to monetary losses to retailers. The economic impact, however, extends beyond the manufacturing and retail industry and affects costs incurred by consumers and taxes lost by the states. Beyond the economic impact, the theft of stolen consumable or health and beauty products may pose safety risks to individuals purchasing such goods from ORC fences. In addition, some industry experts and policy makers have expressed concern about the possibility that proceeds from ORC may be used to fund terrorist activities.

Economic Impact: A Lack of Consensus

The exact loss from organized retail crime to the retail industry is unknown.[42] An often-cited estimate of this loss is $15 billion to $30 billion annually.[43] The original source of this figure, however, has not been identified; while the FBI cites this figure as coming from retail industry estimates,[44] industry experts cite the FBI.[45] As of 2007, the FBI revised the estimated annual loss from ORC and placed it between $30 billion and $37 billion.[46] Of note, these ranges are broad estimates, and it is not precisely evident what the estimated loss includes. On one hand, it may include only the retail value of the merchandise stolen. Alternatively, it may include collateral costs, such as replacement costs or costs for implementing and maintaining various loss prevention measures.

Another unanswered question is whether estimates of losses from ORC include or overlap with estimates of losses from cargo theft. The FBI estimates that cargo theft costs $15 billion to $30 billion annually in the United States.[47] It is not specified, however, what proportion—if any—of cargo theft losses may be attributed to ORC groups. Other estimates have placed the losses from cargo theft at $30 billion to $50 billion annually, with about half of these losses (roughly $15 billion to $25 billion annually) attributed to ORC.[48] If these data are correct, it suggests that the FBI's estimate of cargo theft losses may be largely attributed to either the proportion of cargo theft committed by ORC groups or the proportion of cargo theft not committed by ORC groups. Another explanation may be that industry estimates of losses may differ from law enforcement estimates based on differing criterion for counting an incident as a loss.

The National Retail Security Survey (NRSS) collects data on the levels and causes of inventory "shrinkage"—the reduction in physical inventory caused by shoplifting, employee and vendor theft, and administrative error—as well as data on loss prevention budgets, personnel, and strategies, and responses to shoplifting and employee theft.[49] For the retail sectors surveyed by the NRSS, total sales for 2008 were estimated at $2.4 trillion[50]—about 52% of the total $4.6 trillion annual sales estimated for the entire retail industry.[51]

As outlined in the NRSS, not all retailers are equally susceptible to "shrinkage," and therefore, the NRSS surveys only those sectors that are able to generate "shrinkage" data. [52] Therefore, any conclusions drawn from the NRSS are only generalizable to those retail sectors included in the survey—comprising about 52% of total retail sales.

As illustrated in **Figure 1**, data from the 2008 NRSS indicate that total inventory shrinkage costs amounted to about $36.3 billion in 2008.[53] Of this shrinkage, theft (both internal/employee theft and shoplifting) cost retailers $28.4 billion. In other words, theft accounted for about 78.3% of overall 2008 shrinkage.[54] Within the broad category of theft, internal/employee theft accounted for about $15.5 billion in losses to retailers, and shoplifting led to about $12.9 billion in losses. As mentioned, although retailers estimate that 14.4% of internal theft cases involve collusion with outsiders, it is unknown what proportion (if any) of these involve collusion with organized retail crime groups. With respect to shoplifting cases, retailers have estimated that about 27.5% of shoplifting cases are perpetrated by members of organized retail crime groups. Retailers also indicated that they experienced almost six ORC cases per every $100 million in sales and that the average loss per ORC theft incident averaged to slightly over $5,000.[55]

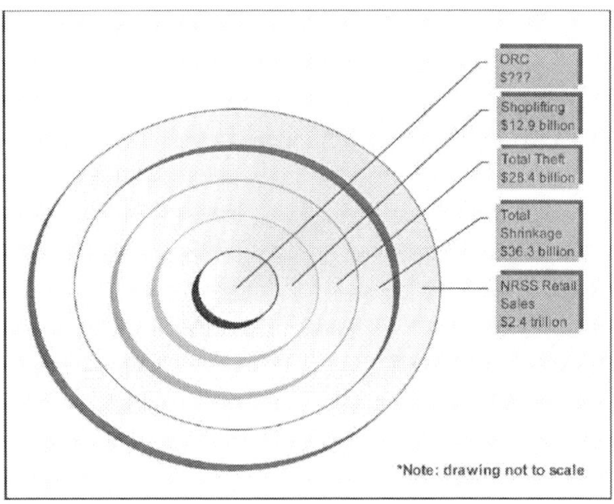

Source: CRS presentation of data from the 2008 National Retail Security Survey Final Report.
Note: This does not include losses to ORC as a result of cargo theft.

Figure 1. 2008 Retail Shrinkage Costs
Costs to retailers participating in the 2008 National Retail Security Survey

As a direct result of retailers' losses to ORC, retailers may take various measures to strengthen retail security and mitigate any financial deficit from the lost revenue. In order to increase merchandise security, prevent future losses, and recoup the lost profits from the retail crime, retailers take measures such as hiring additional loss prevention personnel or increasing the price of goods. These costs are then born by consumers. The price increase may result in some consumers declining to purchase a given product, which may then have a circular effect and result in a loss in sales (and revenue) for the retailers. Retailers may also lock up "hot" products, which, in addition to making the products harder to steal, makes it more difficult for consumers to find and purchase the merchandise. In other cases, the products are simply not available for the customer to purchase because the entire inventory of the product has been stolen.[56]

In addition to the cost of organized retail crime to retailers and consumers, ORC can negatively affect state tax revenue. When goods are stolen rather than purchased, the state does not collect sales tax on the merchandise. The Food Marketing Institute (on behalf of the Coalition Against Organized Retail Crime) estimated that for 2007, the loss of sales tax revenue across the United States totaled about $1.6 billion.[57]

Public Health and Safety Risks

Several of the goods targeted by organized retail crime groups are consumable items or health and beauty products—infant formula, diabetic test strips, and over-the-counter and prescription medications, to name a few. There are public health and safety issues associated with the theft and resale of this merchandise by ORC rings. For instance, after boosters steal perishable goods, these goods may be sold to fencing operations that "clean" the products; as mentioned, this cleaning process may involve repackaging goods (sometimes incorrectly relabeling them) and altering expiration dates before selling the merchandise back to retailers or to the general public. Further, these goods may be stored for indefinite periods of time in trucks or warehouses that are not climate-controlled. These factors may pose risks to the health of people who consume perishable goods that they believe to be safe, but have actually been tampered with or expired.

Potential Links to Terrorism

In addition to the economic and potential public health risks associated with ORC, law enforcement and policy makers have expressed concern that proceeds from organized retail crime may be used to finance terrorist activities.[58] In fact, federal concern over the link between ORC and terrorism was present even before the terrorist attacks of September 11, 2001.[59] Federal law enforcement has traced the illicit proceeds from retail crime, specifically from the theft and resale of infant formula, to terrorist organizations and insurgent groups, including Hamas and Hezbollah.[60] For instance, following the terrorist attacks of 2001, the former U.S. Customs Service established Operation Green Quest—a now-defunct, multi-agency terrorist financing task force—to combat the various sources of terrorist financing; one such source was identified as the "theft, adulteration, and resale of infant formula."[61]

While there may be suspicions that profits from ORC rings have been sent to certain countries to support terrorist activities, it is important to note that no members of ORC rings discussed in the organized retail crime literature have been convicted of providing material support to terrorist organizations. Nevertheless, there are instances in which profits—often from the sale of stolen infant formula—have been transferred to certain countries known to support terrorists, though it has not been determined whether these profits have ultimately been transferred to terrorist organizations.

Three notable investigations of large organized retail crime rings uncovered evidence that the ORC ringleaders had transferred profits from their fencing operations to several countries known to support terrorists. In one case, an investigation into the Jamal Trading Company in Phoenix, AZ, uncovered a money-laundering operation that allegedly funneled the illicit proceeds to countries where several members of the crime ring had ties, such as Iraq, Jordan, and Lebanon. The ringleader, Samih Fadl Jamal, and 15 co-conspirators had been profiting on the sale of stolen infant formula worth $22 million.[62] Another case involved the Ghali organized retail crime ring, led by Mohammed Khalil Ghali, which was involved in the sale of stolen infant formula and other "hot" products, as well as the laundering of the proceeds. An investigation into the Ghali organization found that some of the profits were wired to financial institutions in Jordan, Egypt, and Palestine, and some were smuggled out of the United States on international flights. Further, the Immigration and Customs Enforcement (ICE) has indicated that several members of the Ghali organization allegedly had direct ties to terrorist acts and/or organizations.[63] In a third case, an investigation by the FBI's Joint Terrorism Task Force (JTTF) revealed that the Hamed Organization was a criminal enterprise involved in purchasing and selling stolen and contraband goods, including infant formula, computers, Global Positioning System devices, and cigarettes.[64] Members of the Hamed Organization used convenience stores in which they worked or managed to fence stolen goods and then illegally transferred the proceeds to the Palestinian territories. None of these investigations, however, resulted in defendants being charged with providing material support to terrorists.

There have also been reports of Hamas receiving material support from non-government organizations (NGOs) in the United States, some of which may have received funds from criminal activities such as the sale of stolen infant formula.[65] For instance, it has been suggested that one Muslim charity organization previously operating in the United States, the Holy Land Foundation of Relief and Development (HLF), may have been supported in part by proceeds generated by ORC rings.[66] In 2001, the federal government seized HLF's assets and ordered the organization closed. Five members of HLF were convicted of providing funding, over a period of six years, to Hamas—a specially designated terrorist organization.[67]

As policy makers continue to consider the potential nexus between organized retail crime and terrorism, one important note is that, similar to other organized crime groups, ORC rings are motivated by money. Although this differs from the ideological motivation of terrorist organizations, both organized criminals and terrorists require money.[68] As a means of bringing in this needed income, terrorist groups may model their money-generating criminal activities after those of organized crime groups—including ORC rings. Indeed, federal law enforcement continues to be concerned that organized crime groups may form short-term business partnerships with terrorist organizations if offered enough money.[69]

Current Domestic Efforts to Combat ORC

Retailers

There is a growing awareness among retailers about the consequences of organized retail crime. In its 2010 survey of organized retail crime, the National Retail Federation (NRF) reported that about 90% of the retailers surveyed indicated that their companies had been victimized by ORC, a decrease from the 92% that reported victimization in 2009 but still greater than the 85% that reported victimization in 2008. While the percentage of retailers reporting victimization decreased in 2010, about 59% of all retailers surveyed still reported an increase in ORC activity over the previous year. [70] Further, of the retailers responding to the NRF's 2010 survey, nearly half indicated that they were allocating additional resources to combating ORC.[71] It is unknown, however, whether these trends in *reported* victimization and in *reported* ORC activity levels are clear reflections of *actual* ORC activity or whether these reports are a reflection of the level of attention that retailers pay to ORC.

With the increased knowledge about ORC, nearly 80% of retailers report tracking ORC statistics.[72] Despite this knowledge, however, special ORC task forces have been established only in about 21% of loss prevention departments. Further, even though retailers report an increasing awareness of ORC, the proportion of retailers' funds allocated to loss prevention budgets actually appears to be decreasing; retailers responding to the 2008 NRSS spent an average of 0.34% of their annual sales on loss prevention—a proportion that, prior to 2004, had generally remained above 0.50%.[73]

Retailers' loss prevention strategies can take various different forms, including pre-employment integrity screening measures, employee awareness programs, asset control policies, and loss prevention systems. Data from the 2008 NRSS indicate that over half of retailers use the following loss prevention systems or personnel:

- burglar alarms;
- digital video recording systems;
- live, visible closed circuit TV (CCTV);
- point of sale (POS) data mining software;
- armored car deposit pickups;
- check approval database screening systems;
- live, hidden CCTV;
- secured display fixtures;
- uniformed guards;
- acousto-magnetic, electronic security tags; and
- drop safes.[74]

However, data also indicate that less than half of retailers are using other available loss prevention measures, such as Web-based case management and reporting; cables, locks, and chains; remote CCTV video and audio; observation mirrors; plain-clothed store detectives; and silent alarms.

In addition to their in-house loss prevention measures, some retailers and retail organizations also partner with law enforcement to share information about potential cases of organized retail crime (for more information on these partnerships, see the "Federal Law Enforcement" section). Retailers responding to the 2008 NRSS indicated that almost 54% of ORC investigations were coordinated with local, state, or federal law enforcement. As a result, about 48% of ORC cases were prosecuted.[75]

Online Marketplaces

With an increase in the e-fencing of stolen merchandise, attention has recently turned to the role of Internet marketplaces such as eBay and Overstock in combating ORC. These marketplaces take various measures to combat the sale of stolen and fraudulently obtained goods—not solely by organized retail criminals—on their websites, including educating sellers and consumers, monitoring suspicious activity, and partnering with retailers and law enforcement. For instance, these marketplaces may provide guidelines for website use and require users to acknowledge policies regarding goods that may or may not be sold through the website. In addition, online markets may create filters to search for prohibited items up for auction. They may then take actions such as removing the prohibited items, sanctioning the policy violator, or referring the case to law enforcement. For example, eBay has created such filters based on input from regulatory agencies, law enforcement agencies, the retail industry, and member reports.[76]

Another means by which Internet auction sites may combat the sale of stolen goods is to collaborate with retailers and law enforcement. This could occur through the establishment of investigative task forces or information sharing programs. Of the e-commerce websites most commonly used by criminals to fence stolen goods, eBay claims to be the leader in working with retailers and law enforcement to combat the online sale of stolen goods. For instance, in April 2008, eBay created PROACT (Partnering with Retailers Offensively to Attack Crime and Theft), a program designed to combat the sale of stolen goods on eBay. In this program, retailers voluntarily submit information about potentially stolen or fraudulently obtained goods being sold on eBay. In the first nine months of 2009, retailers brought 415 cases to eBay through the PROACT program.[77] It is unknown, however, how many of these 415 cases may be directly related to organized retail crime. In addition to creating its own programs to combat ORC, eBay partnered with the NRF in

March 2010 to fight this growing crime. The NRF/eBay partnership will utilize PROACT and LERPnet technologies to help track ORC rings, collaborate with the FBI to identify retail crime enterprises, and promote legislation to provide law enforcement with adequate tools to combat ORC thieves.[78]

Federal Law Enforcement

As mentioned, state and local law enforcement have held the primary responsibility for investigating and prosecuting organized retail crime. However, as the scope of the crime has increased, so too has the involvement of federal law enforcement. Retail criminals are no longer selling goods simply at local flea markets; rather, they are using interstate transportation routes to move stolen goods, as well as the Internet to ship this merchandise across the country and around the world.

Much like other forms of organized crime,[79] organized retail crime is becoming increasingly transnational. For law enforcement to effectively combat ORC, it must rely on multilateral coordination, via both domestic and international task forces and partnerships. In addition to expanding multilateral law enforcement partnerships, federal law enforcement has partnered with the retail industry and online markets to combat the theft and illicit resale of stolen goods. Law enforcement has also indicated that it has built cooperative relationships with retailers and online markets and have generally not had trouble obtaining the needed information to investigate potential cases of ORC.[80]

The following section provides a discussion of various federal law enforcement agencies' current efforts to combat organized retail crime.

Federal Bureau of Investigation (FBI)

In December 2003, the FBI established an Organized Retail Theft (ORT) Initiative aimed at identifying and dismantling multi-jurisdictional retail crime rings.[81] The Initiative focuses on information sharing between law enforcement and the private sector in order to investigate ORC and develop a greater understanding of the nature and extent of ORC around the country. The Initiative relies on federal statutes such as the Money Laundering,[82] Interstate Transportation of Stolen Property,[83] and Racketeer Influenced and Corrupt Organizations (RICO)[84] to investigate and prosecute ORC rings. In addition to the Initiative, the FBI leads seven Major Theft Task Forces around the country that are responsible for investigating a host of major theft areas, including ORC. These task forces are composed of local, state, and federal law enforcement agencies, as well as retail industry loss prevention experts.[85]

In the Violence Against Women and Department of Justice Reauthorization Act of 2005, Congress directed the Attorney General and FBI to establish a clearinghouse within the private sector for information sharing between retailers and law enforcement.[86] The result was the Law Enforcement Retail Partnership Network (LERPnet).[87] LERPnet began as a partnership between the FBI, ICE, various local police departments, individual retailers, and retail organizations including the Food Marketing Institute (FMI), National Retail Federation (NRF), and Retail Industry Leaders Association (RILA). As of January, 2010, LERPnet has been linked with the FBI's Law Enforcement Online (LEO) system, providing federal and local law enforcement a direct link to retail industry crime reports.

Despite the establishment of the ORT Initiative, the use of the Major Theft Task Forces to investigate ORC rings, and the creation of LERPnet, the FBI continues to focus most of its resources on counterterrorism efforts. The FBI has indicated that the primary barrier to increasing its involvement in ORC investigations is the lack of resources dedicated directly to combating retail crime. Although the FBI has reportedly requested this directed funding, it has yet to be realized.[88]

U.S. Immigration and Customs Enforcement (ICE)

Because ORC often involves interstate and international transportation of stolen goods and the movement of illicit proceeds associated with the sale of these goods, ICE has become increasingly involved in investigating ORC. Further, ICE may become ever more involved in ORC investigations if reports indicating that ORC rings rely on unauthorized (illegal) aliens[89] (particularly from Mexico) to act as boosters are true.[90] Employing these aliens as low-level boosters allows them to earn an income while protecting the higher-ups in the organization from being apprehended while stealing; if apprehended, unauthorized aliens may be jailed and then deported, saving higher-ups from the fines or jail time that they could otherwise face if arrested.

In July 2009, ICE launched an ORC Pilot Program. This program, originally slated to last for six months in Houston, Los Angeles, Miami, and New York, focused on developing (1) an ORC threat assessment, (2) a tracking system for ORC cases, (3) a database of retail industry contacts to complement the LERPnet database, and (4) an investigation of how ORC groups exploit vulnerabilities in the nation's banking systems to launder illicit proceeds.[91] ICE has indicated that it intends to expand the pilot program into a nation-wide initiative if the results of the program suggest that such an initiative would significantly improve the investigation and prosecution of ORC rings. As of March 2010, the ORC Pilot Program had generated six ORC cases, six criminal arrests, and five convictions.[92] ICE has since extended the program to last an additional 12 months and expanded the program to the National Cyber Crimes Center.[93]

U.S. Secret Service (USSS)

The USSS is most well known for protecting the President and Vice President of the United States, as well as visiting heads of state and government.[94] However, it was originally established as a law enforcement agency charged with investigating and preventing the counterfeiting of U.S. currency. The USSS's authorities have expanded, and the agency now investigates crimes ranging from counterfeiting and financial institution fraud to identity crimes, computer crimes, and money laundering.[95] Through investigations into crimes such as credit card fraud,[96] access device fraud[97] and computer fraud,[98] the USSS has occasionally become involved in investigating organized retail crime groups who steal or fraudulently purchase merchandise from retailers (both traditional and online) and then resell these goods for a profit online.[99] The USSS receives ORC case referrals from state and local law enforcement, retail industry investigators, and online marketplaces fighting the sale of stolen goods.

The USSS has 28 Electronic Fraud Task Forces and 37 Financial Crimes Task Forces that investigate various financial crimes, including ORC.[100] In addition to state and local law enforcement agencies, these task forces consist of investigators from retail stores, online auction houses, and the banking and finance industries. There are an estimated 100 or more retail investigators currently participating in the USSS task forces.

U.S. Postal Inspection Service (USPIS)

The USPIS works to prevent mail fraud as well as illegal substances, contraband, and dangerous products from entering the mail system. When investigating cases of ORC, the USPIS investigates individuals using the mail to ship stolen products or to transmit payment to a seller. These ORC schemes tend to fall into the categories of Internet auction fraud and re-shipper fraud.[101] In cases of Internet auction fraud, the criminals sell stolen goods and ship them domestically and internationally. In cases of re-shipper fraud, criminals may recruit individuals (often unwitting accomplices[102]) to receive the stolen goods and then ship them (often internationally) to other members of the criminal organization or to the buyer of the goods.[103]

Issues for Consideration

When debating the federal government's role in combating organized retail crime, including sanctioning various actors that may be involved in committing or aiding these crimes, there are several issues that policy makers may consider. One is whether retailers are taking sufficient preventative measures to prevent retail theft. Another issue is whether criminalizing organized retail crime at the federal level would allow for more effective investigation and prosecution of these criminals. Yet another issue is whether regulating online marketplaces to require that such entities increase information sharing with retailers and law enforcement would improve investigations and prosecutions of ORC as well as decrease the prevalence of retail thieves fencing stolen goods via legitimate online marketplaces.

Are Retailers Doing Enough?

The first line of defense against organized retail crime is preventing the crimes from ever occurring. This involves security at the manufacturing sites, distribution centers, retail stores, and in the transportation throughout this supply chain.[104] The NRSS present trends in retail industry loss prevention measures since 1991. The 2008 NRSS reports that retailers spent 0.34% of annual sales on loss prevention measures such as contract services, security equipment, and loss prevention personnel.[105] This includes about 140 loss prevention employees for every $100 million in annual sales.[106] As mentioned, prior to 2004, the percent of annual sales spent on loss prevention was consistently above 0.50%, but that amount has been decreasing over the past several years. Some experts explain this decrease in the loss prevention budget as a reaction to declines in overall inventory shrinkage over the past several years.[107] Despite this general decline in shrinkage rates, 59% of retailers surveyed have seen an increase in ORC activity.[108] Another explanation for the average decline in loss prevention budgets may stem from the recent economic downturn if retailers scaled back on loss prevention measures in order to save on costs. CRS was unable to locate data, however, on whether retailers are not spending on loss prevention because they cannot afford to or because they choose not to spend in this area.

For multiple reasons, it is difficult to empirically determine whether retailers are doing "enough" to combat ORC. For one, retailers must strike a balance between protecting their merchandise from thieves and creating an environment where honest consumers can easily find and purchase the desired products. If retailers take every precaution to lock up "hot" products and install security measures that make it difficult for consumers to get the desired product in a hassle-free and timely fashion, they may risk losing customers to competitors who provide a more relaxed shopping environment. If, on the other hand, retailers err on the side of being "customer friendly" by keeping products out in the open, they may open themselves up to thieves.

There are several policy options that may enhance retailers' abilities to combat ORC that policy makers may consider. In the literature, there appears to be a lack of research on the effectiveness of various loss prevention strategies on combating retail theft in general and ORC in particular. Understanding the strategies that have proven to reduce retail theft related to ORC may enhance retailers' abilities to secure their merchandise. Consequently, one option may be for Congress to commission a national study to examine promising loss prevention strategies. A second option may be for Congress to consider establishing a grant program that would provide funding to retailers to install or upgrade security systems and loss prevention measures in their stores. Congress could require that retailers comply with various benchmarks in order to receive grant funding; for instance, a grant program may require that retailers work with law enforcement to identify and apprehend members of ORC rings. Another potential requirement could be that retailers join LERPnet in order to be eligible for grant funding. Yet another eligibility requirement could be that retailers provide matching loss prevention funds.

Federally Criminalizing ORC

Combating retail theft has primarily been handled by state law enforcement under state criminal laws. In particular, major theft laws are the statutes that states have relied upon most to investigate and prosecute ORC. These major theft laws, however, vary from state to state with respect to the monetary threshold that constitutes major theft.[109] While some states, such as New Jersey and Massachusetts, have relatively low thresholds, other states, such as Wisconsin and Pennsylvania, have relatively higher thresholds. Over one-third of states have felony theft thresholds that meet or exceed $1,000. With respect to organized retail crime, 16 states have passed legislation criminalizing ORC, and 8 others have pending legislation.[110]

There is currently no federal law specifically prohibiting organized retail crime as such. There are, however, provisions in the *U.S. Code* that federal law enforcement uses to bring forth cases against ORC rings. Examples of such provisions include

- 18 U.S.C. § 1956, "Laundering of monetary instruments";
- 18 U.S.C. § 1957, "Engaging in monetary transactions in property derived from specified unlawful activity";
- 18 U.S.C., Chapter 96, the Racketeer Influenced and Corrupt Organizations (RICO) provisions;
- 18 U.S.C. § 2314, "Transportation of stolen goods, securities, moneys, fraudulent State tax stamps, or articles used in counterfeiting"; and
- 18 U.S.C. § 2315, "Sale or receipt of stolen goods, securities, moneys, or fraudulent State tax stamps."

Current federal law addressing theft does not criminalize the theft itself, but rather prohibits the transportation of stolen goods across state lines[111] as well as the sale or receipt of these goods.[112] For these activities to be considered federal crimes, the monetary value of the stolen goods must meet or exceed $5,000.

When debating the federal government's role in combating organized retail crime, Congress may consider whether current law should be amended to create new provisions that would provide penalties for ORC. [113] Proponents of such legislation argue that criminalizing ORC may benefit law enforcement in several ways, including (1) illuminating the growing problem of ORC and (2) providing a statutory framework for tracking ORC case data rather than lumping these cases into other categories for statistical purposes. Opponents of legislation criminalizing ORC argue that already existing statutes allow for effective investigation and prosecution of ORC (as outlined above) and that creating a separate provision for ORC would be redundant. Representatives from federal law enforcement agencies have provided congressional testimony indicating that they indeed have sufficient laws and procedural tools to investigate ORC.[114] As mentioned, impediments to investigating and prosecuting these cases may come more from a lack of resources than from a need for better investigative and prosecutorial tools.

Another policy option that Congress may consider could be enacting provisions that would lower the monetary threshold from $5,000 for the sale, receipt, or transportation of stolen goods across state lines (18 U.S.C. § 2314 and 18 U.S.C. § 2315).[115] Currently, the highest state felony theft level is $2,500, and the average is slightly over $700.[116] Savvy criminals know each state's felony theft level and steal merchandise valuing just under this level so as to avoid state felony charges if caught. Federal investigators and prosecutors may rely upon the sum total of merchandise stolen in various states and moved across state lines in order to prosecute these thieves. The average value of goods transported, sold, or received by members of ORC rings is currently unknown. If this value were under the current federal threshold of $5,000, the data may support legislation decreasing the threshold. One issue that Congress may face if it amends the $5,000 limit for the sale, receipt, or transportation of stolen goods across state lines may be whether such a policy shift would also open the doors for the federal government to prosecute individuals not involved in ORC rings.

If Congress determines that there are sufficient investigative and prosecutorial tools available for law enforcement to combat ORC, one issue that policy makers may face is whether to provide dedicated funding to law enforcement to enhance their ability to take on more ORC cases. Law enforcement has suggested that although the investigative tools are available, it may prioritize and utilize resources in higher-priority areas[117]—such as counterterrorism and fraud investigations.[118] Therefore, another policy option may be to provide directed resources to federal law enforcement to investigate and prosecute ORC cases.

Regulation of Online and Physical Marketplaces

As mentioned, organized retail criminals use both physical and online marketplaces as fences to sell stolen goods. With an increasingly globalized society, these criminals take advantage of the Internet for their illegal activities. In an effort to curb sales of stolen goods online, one policy option that Congress may consider is increased regulation of certain actions on the Internet. In the past, Congress has regulated actions on the Internet that involve interstate commerce. For example, Congress enacted legislation that prohibited unlawful Internet gambling.[119] Among other things, this legislation also included provisions holding certain computer services, Internet websites, telecommunications services, and financial transaction providers liable for illegal gambling if they aid or have knowledge of the Internet gambling.[120] Along the same lines, Congress may consider whether to regulate online auction websites to require them to document, retain, and disclose—to designated law enforcement—information about specified sellers, including those suspected of fencing stolen goods. Proponents of such regulation argue that this could better enable law enforcement to track suspected fences and that it may act as a deterrent, discouraging potential thieves from fencing stolen goods.[121] Opponents of this type of regulation argue that online marketplaces already share such information because it is in their best interests to prevent the sale of stolen goods, promote the business of legitimate sellers, and ensure that customers receive genuine and safe products.

Another policy option that policy makers may consider is the regulation of physical marketplaces, such as flea markets. One the one hand, some may argue that flea markets should be regulated by state laws because the face-to-face transactions at these markets do not directly involve interstate commerce. Others, however, may contend that the federal government could regulate the goods sold at flea markets because they were likely involved in interstate commerce before being sold at the market. Further, it could be argued that the federal government could direct this regulation toward the sale of certain, already-regulated products such as goods regulated by the Food and Drug Administration (FDA) under the Federal Food, Drug, and Cosmetics Act.[122]

APPENDIX. STATE FELONY THEFT LEVELS

Table A-1. State Felony Theft Levels

State	Felony Theft Level (in dollars)
Alabama	500
Alaska	500
Arizona	1,000
Arkansas	500
California	400
Colorado	500
Connecticut	1,000

Table A-1. (Continued)

State	Felony Theft Level (in dollars)
Delaware	1,000
Florida	300
Georgia	300
Hawaii	300
Idaho	1,000
Illinois	150
Indiana	Any[a]
Iowa	1,000
Kansas	1,000
Kentucky	500
Louisiana	500
Maine	1,000
Maryland	1,000
Massachusetts	250
Michigan	1,000
Minnesota	500
Mississippi	500
Missouri	500
Montana	1,000
Nebraska	500
Nevada	250
New Hampshire	500
New Jersey	250
New Mexico	500
New York	1,000
North Carolina	1,000
North Dakota	500
Ohio	500
Oklahoma	500
Oregon	750
Pennsylvania	2,000
Rhode Island	500
South Carolina	1,000
South Dakota	500
Tennessee	500

Table A-1. (Continued)

State	Felony Theft Level (in dollars)
Texas	1,500
Utah	1,000
Vermont	900
Virginia	200
Washington	750
Washington, DC	250
West Virginia	1,000
Wisconsin	2,500
Wyoming	1,000
Federal[b]	5,000

Source: CRS presentation of data provided by Frank Muscato, Walgreens ORC Investigations Supervisor, November 9, 2009.

a. In Indiana, theft is always a Class D felony, regardless of amount.

b. The federal law addressing theft does not criminalize theft itself, but rather prohibits the transportation of stolen goods across state lines (18 U.S.C. § 2314) as well as the sale or receipt of these goods (18 U.S.C. § 2315).

End Notes

[1] A "booster" is someone who steals merchandise and then sells it to a fence for a profit. A "fence" is someone who knowingly buys illegally obtained goods from a "booster" and then sells the goods for a profit.

[2] Ticket switching involves thieves utilizing devices that create fake barcodes that they adhere to packages, covering the original barcodes. When scanned, these new barcodes ring up items at lower prices than their retail values.

[3] See the National Retail Federation, *2010 Organized Retail Crime Survey*, 2010, p. 5. The percentage of surveyed retailers who reported victimization generally increased between 2005 and 2009 and then decreased slightly in 2010.

[4] Issues involved in determining the exact losses are discussed later in the report. The National Retail Federation (NRF) has estimated that losses amass to between $15 billion and $30 billion annually. The Federal Bureau of Investigation (FBI) has provided varying estimates. In 2005, the FBI cited losses as between $15 billion and $30 billion annually. See testimony of Chris Swecker, Assistant Director, Criminal Investigative Division, Federal Bureau of Investigation before the U.S. Congress, House Committee on the Judiciary, Subcommittee on Crime, Terrorism, and Homeland Security, *Responding to Organized Crimes Against Manufacturers and Retailers*, 109th Cong., 1st sess., March 17, 2005. As of 2007, the FBI estimated losses as between $30 billion and $37 billion annually. See the Federal Bureau of Investigation, *Organized Retail Theft: New Initiative to Tackle the Problem*, April 6, 2007, http://www.fbi.gov/page2/ april07/retail040607.htm.

[5] See testimony of Chris Swecker, Assistant Director, Criminal Investigative Division, Federal Bureau of Investigation before the U.S. Congress, House Committee on the Judiciary,

Subcommittee on Crime, Terrorism, and Homeland Security, *Responding to Organized Crimes Against Manufacturers and Retailers*, 109th Cong., 1st sess., March 17, 2005.

[6] Charles I. Miller, *Organized Retail Theft: Raising Awareness, Offering Solutions*, National Retail Federation Foundation, 2005, p. 4. See also Food Marketing Institute, *Media Reports—Middle East Connection: Organized Retail Crime*, *http://www.fm* i.org/docs/loss/ORCMiddleEast.pdf. See also testimony by David Johnson, Section Chief, Criminal Investigative Division, Federal Bureau of Investigation, before the U.S. Congress, House Committee on the Judiciary, Subcommittee on Crime, Terrorism, and Homeland Security, *Combating Organized Retail Crime: The Role of Federal Law Enforcement*, 111th Cong., 1st sess., November 5, 2009.

[7] From a statement by Representative Robert C. "Bobby" Scott before the U.S. Congress, House Committee on the Judiciary, Subcommittee on Crime, Terrorism, and Homeland Security, *E-Fencing Enforcement Act of 2008, The Organized Retail Crime Act of 2008, and The Combating Organized Retail Crime Act of 2008*, 110th Cong., 2nd sess., September 22, 2008.

[8] See **Appendix** for a table displaying felony theft levels by state.

[9] Walter E. Palmer and Chris Richardson, *Organized Retail Crime: Assessing the Risk and Developing Effective Strategies*, ASIS Foundation Research Council, 2009, p. 4.

[10] For statistical purposes, the FBI defines cargo theft as "the criminal taking of any cargo including, but not limited to, goods, chattels, money, or baggage that constitutes, in whole or in part, a commercial shipment of freight moving in commerce, from any pipeline system, railroad car, motortruck, or other vehicle, or from any tank or storage facility, station house, platform, or depot, or from any vessel or wharf, or from any aircraft, air terminal, airport, aircraft terminal or air navigation facility, or from any intermodal container, intermodal chassis, trailer, container freight station, warehouse, freight distribution facility, or freight consolidation facility. For purposes of this definition, cargo shall be deemed as moving in commerce at all points between the point of origin and the final destination, regardless of any temporary stop while awaiting transshipment or otherwise." U.S. Department of Justice, Federal Bureau of Investigation, Criminal Justice Information Services Division, Uniform Crime Reporting Program, *National Incident-Based Reporting System Addendum for Submitting Cargo Theft Data*, January 2010, p. iii, http://www.fbi.gov/ucr/ nibrs/downloadables/nibrs_cargo_theft_downloadable.pdf.

[11] See, for example, Read Hayes, *Organized Retail Crime Annual Report 2008: Describing a Major Problem*, Loss Prevention Research Council, 2008, hereafter *Organized Retail Crime Annual Report 2008: Describing a Major Problem*. The issue of cargo theft will be discussed in more detail in the section, "Methods Used by Boosters."

[12] See, for example, Walter E. Palmer and Chris Richardson, *Organized Retail Crime: Assessing the Risk and Developing Effective Strategies*, ASIS Foundation Research Council, 2009.

[13] *Organized Retail Crime Annual Report 2008: Describing a Major Problem.*

[14] This issue is discussed further in the section "Domestic Impact of Organized Retail Crime."

[15] P.L. 109-162, § 1105, codified at 28 U.S.C. § 509 note. In the Violence Against Women and Department of Justice Reauthorization Act of 2005, Congress defined organized retail theft and directed the Attorney General and FBI to establish a task force to combat organized retail theft as well as a clearinghouse within the private sector for information sharing between retailers and law enforcement.

[16] Charles I. Miller, *Organized Retail Theft: Raising Awareness, Offering Solutions*, National Retail Federation Foundation, 2005, p. 17.

[17] Ibid.

[18] Ibid., pp. 17-20. The public health and safety risks and possible repercussions of these cleaning operations are discussed elsewhere in this chapter.

[19] Ronald V. Clarke, "Hot Products: Understanding, Anticipating, and Reducing Demand for Stolen Goods," *Police Research Series*, Paper 112 (1999), p. 23.

[20] Ibid., p. 1.

[21] *Organized Retail Crime Annual Report 2008: Describing a Major Problem,* p. 20. Benadryl, for instance, has been identified as one of the over-the-counter medications targeted by ORC groups, where competing brands of antihistamines have not.

[22] Ibid.

[23] Read Hayes and King Rogers, "Catch Them if You Can: This Study of Organized Retail Crime Looks at How These Criminal Groups Operate and What Measures Might Help Stores Fight Back," *Security Management*, vol. 47, no. 10 (2003), hereafter "Catch Them if You Can."

[24] Ibid.

[25] From information provided to CRS during an organized retail crime briefing by members of the Retail Leaders Industry Association and the Coalition Against Organized Retail Crime, June 4, 2009.

[26] "Catch Them if You Can."

[27] Ibid.

[28] Richard C. Hollinger and Amanda Adams, *2008 National Retail Security Survey Final Report*, Security Research Project, Department of Sociology and Criminology & Law, University of Florida, 2009, p. 7, hereafter *2008 National Retail Security Survey Final Report.*

[29] Ibid., pp. 7-8. In addition to employees colluding with ORC thieves, they may also conspire with individuals to steal merchandise for personal use—either for the employees' own use or for the co-conspirators' use.

[30] From information provided to CRS during an organized retail crime briefing by members of the Retail Leaders Industry Association and the Coalition Against Organized Retail Crime, June 4, 2009.

[31] Ibid.

[32] Ibid.

[33] *Organized Retail Crime Annual Report 2008: Describing a Major Problem,* pp. 17-18.

[34] Ibid., Walter E. Palmer and Chris Richardson, *Organized Retail Crime: Assessing the Risk and Developing Effective Strategies*, ASIS Foundation Research Council, 2009, p. 14.

[35] Tracy Johnson and Read Hayes, "Behind the Fence: Buying and Selling Stolen Merchandise," *Security Journal*, vol. 16, no. 4 (2003).

[36] *Organized Retail Crime Annual Report 2008: Describing a Major Problem.*

[37] King Rogers, "Organized Retail Theft," in *Retail Crime, Security, and Loss Prevention: An Encyclopedic Reference*, ed. Charles A. Sennewald and John H. Christman (Elseiver Inc., 2008).

[38] National Retail Federation, *2010 Organized Retail Crime Survey*, 2010, p. 7.

[39] Ibid., p. 9.

[40] National Retail Federation, *2009 Organized Retail Crime Survey*, 2009, p. 8.

[41] See, for example, testimony of Brad Brekke, Vice President of Assets Protection, Target Corporation, before the U.S. Congress, House Committee on the Judiciary, Subcommittee on Crime, Terrorism, and Homeland Security, *Organized Retail Theft Prevention: Fostering a Comprehensive Public-Private Response*, 110th Cong., 1st sess., October 25, 2007, H.Hrg. 110-122.

[42] Walter E. Palmer and Chris Richardson, *Organized Retail Crime: Assessing the Risk and Developing Effective Strategies*, ASIS Foundation Research Council, 2009, p. 5.

[43] See, for example, testimony of Chris Swecker, Assistant Director, Criminal Investigative Division, Federal Bureau of Investigation before the U.S. Congress, House Committee on the Judiciary, Subcommittee on Crime, Terrorism, and Homeland Security, *Responding to Organized Crimes Against Manufacturers and Retailers*, 109th Cong., 1st sess., March 17, 2005.

[44] Ibid.

[45] Testimony of Karl Langhorst, Director of Loss Prevention, Randall's/Tom Thumb, a Safeway Company before the U.S. Congress, House Committee on the Judiciary, Subcommittee on Crime, Terrorism, and Homeland Security, *Organized Retail Theft: Fostering a Comprehensive Public-Private Response*, 111th Cong., 2nd sess., October 25, 2007.

[46] Federal Bureau of Investigation, *Organized Retail Theft: New Initiative to Tackle the Problem*, April 6, 2007, http://www.fbi.gov/page2/april07/retail040607.htm.

[47] Federal Bureau of Investigation, *Cargo Theft's High Cost: Thieves Stealing Billions Annually*, July 21, 2006, http://www.fbi.gov/page2/july06/cargo_theft072106.htm.

[48] As cited by Claire Mayhew, "The Detection and Prevention of Cargo Theft," *Trends & Issues in Crime and Criminal Justice*, no. 214 (September 2001), p. 1.

[49] *2008 National Retail Security Survey Final Report.*

[50] *2008 National Retail Security Survey Final Report*, p. 6.

[51] National Retail Federation, *2009 Organized Retail Crime Survey*, 2009, p. 2.

[52] The NRSS surveyed retailers from the following sectors: optical; children's apparel; strip center; women's apparel; discount store; crafts and hobbies; men's and women's apparel; entertainment, media, games, video, and music; sporting goods and recreational products; shoes; department store; accessories; supermarket and grocery; household furnishings and housewares; cards, gifts, floral, and novelties; office supplies; stationery; books, magazines, and music; drug store; homecenter, hardware, lumber, and garden; electronics, computers, and appliances; and furniture. Of note, the NRSS does not include data from retailers such as restaurants, bars, motor vehicle dealers, auto service stations, direct catalog sale outlets, and Internet "e-tailers" because these sectors do not produce comparable "shrinkage" data to the other retailers that are included in the survey.

[53] *2008 National Retail Security Survey Final Report*, p. 6.

[54] The other known sources of shrinkage were administrative errors and vendor fraud.

[55] *2008 National Retail Security Survey Final Report*, p. 30.

[56] From information provided to CRS during an organized retail crime briefing by members of the Retail Leaders Industry Association and the Coalition Against Organized Retail Crime, June 4, 2009.

[57] Food Marketing Institute, on behalf of the Coalition Against Organized Retail Crime, *Organized Retail Crime: Estimated Lost Sales Tax Revenue by State (2007)*, September 2009. The most recent data available comes from 2007.

[58] See testimony of Chris Swecker, Assistant Director, Criminal Investigative Division, Federal Bureau of Investigation before the U.S. Congress, House Committee on the Judiciary, Subcommittee on Crime, Terrorism, and Homeland Security, *Responding to Organized Crimes Against Manufacturers and Retailers*, 109th Cong., 1st sess., March 17, 2005.

[59] Karen E. Thuermer, "Retailers Organize Against Crime," *Security Management*, July 2007.

[60] Charles I. Miller, *Organized Retail Theft: Raising Awareness, Offering Solutions*, National Retail Federation Foundation, 2005, p. 4. See also Food Marketing Institute, *Media Reports—Middle East Connection: Organized Retail Crime*, *http://www.fmi.org/do* cs/loss/ORCMiddleEast.pdf. See also testimony by David Johnson, Section Chief, Criminal Investigative Division, Federal Bureau of Investigation, before the U.S. Congress, House Committee on the Judiciary, Subcommittee on Crime, Terrorism, and Homeland Security, *Combating Organized Retail Crime: The Role of Federal Law Enforcement*, 111th Cong., 1st sess., November 5, 2009.

[61] U.S. Department of the Treasury, U.S. Customs Service, Office of Investigations, *Green Quest*, Customs Publication No. 0000-0171, October 2002, p. 2, *http://www.porta* l.state.pa.us/portal/server.pt/document/437021/green_quest_brochure_pdf.

[62] Charles I. Miller, *Organized Retail Theft: Raising Awareness, Offering Solutions*, National Retail Federation Foundation, 2005, pp. 25 - 27.

[63] Testimony by Janice Ayala, Assistant Director for Investigative Programs, Office of Investigations, U.S. Immigration and Customs Enforcement, Department of Homeland Security, before the U.S. Congress, House Committee on the Judiciary, Subcommittee on Crime, Terrorism, and Homeland Security, *Combating Organized Retail Crime: The Role of Federal Law Enforcement*, 111th Cong., 1st sess., November 5, 2009.

[64] United States Attorney's Office Eastern District of Missouri, "Eight Area Men Plead Guilty to Federal Racketeering Charges Involving Conspiracy to Transfer Cash and Checks to the

Palestinian Territories," press release, November 24, 2009, http://stlouis.fbi.gov/dojpressrel/pressrel09/sl112409a.htm.

[65] From testimony by John S. Pistole, Assistant Director, Counterterrorism Division, Federal Bureau of Investigation, before the U.S. Congress, House Committee on Financial Services, Subcommittee on Oversight and Investigations, *Hamas Asset Freeze and Other Government Efforts To Stop Terrorist Funding*, 108th Cong., 1st sess., September 24, 2003.

[66] Charles I. Miller, *Organized Retail Theft: Raising Awareness, Offering Solutions*, National Retail Federation Foundation, 2005, pp. 12 – 13.

[67] In November, 2008, a federal jury returned convictions for five members of the HLF accused of providing about $12.4 million in material support to Hamas. For more information, see http://www.fbi.gov/page2/nov08/ hlf_112508.html and *http://www.justice.gov/opa/pr/2008/November/08-nsd-1046.html*.

[68] For more information on the potential links between organized crime in the United States and terrorist organizations, see CRS Report R40525, *Organized Crime in the United States: Trends and Issues for Congress*, by Kristin M. Finklea.

[69] Pat Milton, "FBI Worries About an Osama-Sopranos Link," *Associated Press*, October 1, 2006, http://www.redorbit.com/news/general/676652/ fbi_worries_about_an_ osamas opranos_ link/index.html. See also *Mapping the Global Structure*, National Intelligence Council, Report of the National Intelligence Council's 2020 Project, Based on consultations with nongovernmental experts around the world, Washington, D.C., December 2004, p. 96.

[70] National Retail Federation, *2010 Organized Retail Crime Survey*, 2010, p. 5.

[71] Ibid., p. 6. Of the retailers responding to the NRF's 2009 survey, the average annual labor costs spent to combat ORC was $215,000, and 6% of these retailers spent over $1 million annually.

[72] *2008 National Retail Security Survey Final Report*, p. 30.

[73] Ibid., p. 12. There are various explanations for the decrease in the proportion of sales spent on loss prevention. For instance, one possibility is that an increase in total sales was not met with a relative increase in loss prevention measures. While overall sales may have climbed (as is suggested by 2008 U.S. Department of Commerce Retail Industry Census data), it is unknown whether loss prevention budgets increased, decreased, or remained the same.

[74] Ibid., pp. 23-25.

[75] *2008 National Retail Security Survey Final Report*, p. 30.

[76] From information provided to CRS during ORC briefing by representatives from eBay on July 27, 2009.

[77] Information from correspondence between eBay and CRS, October 2, 2009.

[78] National Retail Federation, "National Retail Federation, eBay Announce Partnership to Fight Organized Retail Crime," press release, March 22, 2010, *http://www.nrf.com/modules.php?name=News&op=viewlive&sp_id=906*.

[79] For further information on organized crime, see CRS Report R40525, *Organized Crime in the United States: Trends and Issues for Congress*, by Kristin M. Finklea.

[80] Testimony by law enforcement representatives from the FBI, ICE, USSS, and USPIS before the U.S. Congress, House Committee on the Judiciary, Subcommittee on Crime, Terrorism, and Homeland Security, *Combating Organized Retail Crime: The Role of Federal Law Enforcement*, 111th Cong., 1st sess., November 5, 2009. Also from an ICE briefing for CRS, October 14, 2009 and a USSS briefing for CRS, November 13, 2009.

[81] The FBI utilizes the term ORT rather than ORC so as not to create a confusion between organized retail crime and traditional organized crime.

[82] 18 U.S.C. § 1956.

[83] 18 U.S.C. § 2314.

[84] 18 U.S.C., Chapter 96.

[85] Testimony by David Johnson, Section Chief, Criminal Investigative Division, Federal Bureau of Investigation, before the U.S. Congress, House Committee on the Judiciary,

Subcommittee on Crime, Terrorism, and Homeland Security, *Combating Organized Retail Crime: The Role of Federal Law Enforcement*, 111th Cong., 1st sess., November 5, 2009.

[86] P.L. 109-162, § 1105, codified at 28 U.S.C. § 509 note.

[87] For more information on LERPnet, see http://www.lerpnet.com/.

[88] Testimony by David Johnson, Section Chief, Criminal Investigative Division, Federal Bureau of Investigation, before the U.S. Congress, House Committee on the Judiciary, Subcommittee on Crime, Terrorism, and Homeland Security, *Combating Organized Retail Crime: The Role of Federal Law Enforcement*, 111th Cong., 1st sess., November 5, 2009.

[89] An alien is anyone who is not a citizen or national of the United States and is synonymous with non-citizen.

[90] See, for example, Charles I. Miller, *Organized Retail Theft: Raising Awareness, Offering Solutions*, National Retail Federation Foundation, 2005, p. 1. Some have suggested that unauthorized aliens may be particularly vulnerable to being recruited by ORC groups because they are looking to earn money while in the United States and may be seen as expendable by higher-ups in the organization.

[91] Testimony by Janice Ayala, Assistant Director for Investigative Programs, Office of Investigations, U.S. Immigration and Customs Enforcement, Department of Homeland Security, before the U.S. Congress, House Committee on the Judiciary, Subcommittee on Crime, Terrorism, and Homeland Security, *Combating Organized Retail Crime: The Role of Federal Law Enforcement*, 111th Cong., 1st sess., November 5, 2009.

[92] Information provided to CRS by ICE, March 19, 2010.

[93] See the National Retail Federation, *2010 Organized Retail Crime Survey*, 2010, p. 11. For more information on the National Cyber Crimes Center, see http://www.ice.gov/partners/investigations/services/cyberbranch.htm.

[94] See http://www.secretservice.gov/investigations.shtml.

[95] According to the USSS, "investigations include counterfeiting of U.S. currency (to include coins); counterfeiting of foreign currency (occurring domestically); identity crimes such as access device fraud, identity theft, false identification fraud, bank fraud and check fraud; telemarketing fraud; telecommunications fraud (cellular and hard wire); computer fraud; fraud targeting automated payment systems and teller machines; direct deposit fraud; investigations of forgery, uttering, alterations, false impersonations or false claims involving U.S. Treasury Checks, U.S. Saving Bonds, U.S. Treasury Notes, Bonds and Bills; electronic funds transfer (EFT) including Treasury disbursements and fraud within the Treasury payment systems; Federal Deposit Insurance Corporation investigations; Farm Credit Administration violations; and fictitious or fraudulent commercial instruments and foreign securities." For more information, see http://www.secretservice.gov/criminal.shtml.

[96] 18 U.S.C. § 1029(a)(10).

[97] 18 U.S.C. § 1029.

[98] 18 U.S.C. § 1030.

[99] USSS briefing for CRS, November 13, 2009.

[100] Ibid., See also testimony by John R. Large, Special Agent in Charge, Criminal Investigative Division, Office of Investigations, U.S. Secret Service before the U.S. Congress, House Committee on the Judiciary, Subcommittee on Crime, Terrorism, and Homeland Security, *Combating Organized Retail Crime: The Role of Federal Law Enforcement*, 111th Cong., 1st sess., November 5, 2009.

[101] Testimony of Zane M. Hill, Deputy Chief Postal Inspector, U.S. Postal Inspection Service before the U.S. Congress, House Committee on the Judiciary, Subcommittee on Crime, Terrorism, and Homeland Security, *Combating Organized Retail Crime: The Role of Federal Law Enforcement*, 111th Cong., 1st sess., November 5, 2009.

[102] One common method of recruiting these unwitting accomplices is through employment websites where the criminals advertise work-from-home jobs as shippers.

[103] For more information on re-shipping scams, see https://postalinspectors.uspis.gov/radDocs/consumer/ ReshippingScam.html.

[104] Detailed information on retailers' efforts to combat ORC is provided in the "Retailers" section of this chapter.

[105] *2008 National Retail Security Survey Final Report*, p. 12.

[106] Ibid., p. 15.

[107] Ibid., p. 12.

[108] As mentioned, the NRF's 2010 survey of retailers reports that about 90% of the retailers surveyed indicated that their companies had been victimized by ORC, a decrease over the 92% that reported victimization in 2009, but an increase over the 85% that reported victimization in 2008. While the overall percentage of retailers reporting ORC victimization decreased in 2010, a majority (59%) of surveyed retailers still reported an increase in ORC activity. See National Retail Federation, *2010 Organized Retail Crime Survey*, 2010.

[109] See the **Appendix** for a table displaying felony theft levels by state.

[110] From an organized retail crime and felony theft level database maintained and provided to CRS by Frank Muscato, ORC Investigations Supervisor, Organized Retail Crime Division, Walgreens, November 9, 2009.

[111] 18 U.S.C. § 2314.

[112] 18 U.S.C. § 2315.

[113] The Organized Retail Crime Act of 2009 (H.R. 1173) would, among other things, define and criminalize ORC. It would also modify the transportation of stolen goods as well as the sale and receipt of stolen goods statutes to include ORC. Similarly, the Organized Retail Crime Prevention and Enforcement Act of 2009 (H.R. 4011) would expand these statutes to criminalize the transportation to and sale of goods (that were stolen or fraudulently obtained) on an online marketplace.

[114] Testimony by law enforcement representatives from the FBI, ICE, USSS, and USPIS before the U.S. Congress, House Committee on the Judiciary, Subcommittee on Crime, Terrorism, and Homeland Security, *Combating Organized Retail Crime: The Role of Federal Law Enforcement*, 111th Cong., 1st sess., November 5, 2009.

[115] The Organized Retail Crime Prevention and Enforcement Act of 2009 (H.R. 4011) would, among other things, lower the monetary threshold to $1,000 for the sale, receipt, and transportation of stolen goods across state lines. The Combating Organized Retail Crime Act of 2009 (S. 470) would amend the statutes to criminalize the sale, receipt, or transportation of stolen goods having an aggregate value of $5,000 or more during any 12-month period.

[116] See the **Appendix** for a table displaying felony theft levels by state.

[117] Testimony by David Johnson, Section Chief, Criminal Investigative Division, Federal Bureau of Investigation, before the U.S. Congress, House Committee on the Judiciary, Subcommittee on Crime, Terrorism, and Homeland Security, *Combating Organized Retail Crime: The Role of Federal Law Enforcement*, 111th Cong., 1st sess., November 5, 2009.

[118] Testimony by Robert S. Mueller, III, Director, Federal Bureau of Investigation, before the U.S. Congress, Senate Committee on the Judiciary, *Oversight of the Federal Bureau of Investigation*, 111th Cong., 1st sess., September 16, 2009.

[119] See 18 U.S.C. § 1084 and Title VIII of P.L. 109-347, Unlawful Internet Gambling Enforcement, codified at 31 U.S.C. § 5361 et seq.

[120] See 31 U.S.C. § 5365 - 5366.

[121] The E-fencing Enforcement Act of 2009 (H.R. 1166) would, among other things, require online marketplaces to disclose to law enforcement the contact information of high volume sellers who are selling goods matching law enforcement's description of stolen goods. Also, the Organized Retail Crime Act of 2009 (H.R. 1173) would, among other things, require online marketplaces to investigate credible claims of stolen goods (obtained and sold via ORC) being sold on their websites. It would also necessitate such marketplaces to require that high-volume sellers make available contact information and information about the source of the products sold.

[122] 21 U.S.C. § 301.

In: Organized Retail Crime
Editors: Blake H. Liventin
ISBN: 978-1-61122-768-0

Chapter 2

STATEMENT OF DAVID JOHNSON, SECTION CHIEF, CRIMINAL INVESTIGATIVE DIVISION, FEDERAL BUREAU OF INVESTIGATION, BEFORE THE UNITED STATES HOUSE JUDICIARY SUBCOMMITTEE ON CRIME, TERRORISM, AND HOMELAND SECURITY

Good morning, Chairman Scott, Ranking Member Gohmert and Members of the Subcommittee. I appreciate the opportunity to testify before you today on the FBI's efforts to combat organized retail theft (ORT) in the United States. We prefer to use the term "organized retail theft" because the term "organized crime" has a specific meaning within the context of law enforcement. Therefore referring to the criminal activity as "organized retail crime" creates confusion.

ORT THREAT

What is called Organized Retail Theft or ORT by Retail Loss Prevention Professionals, can generally be described as professional burglars, boosters, cons, thieves, fences and resellers conspiring to steal and sell retail merchandise obtained from retail establishments by theft or deception. 'Boosters' – the front line thieves who intend to resell stolen goods – generally coordinate with 'fences' who may sell the items outright at flea markets or convenience stores or online; or repackage them for sale to higher level fences. The problem is significant for its negative economic impact, the safety issues it brings to unsuspecting consumers, and its potential link to other criminal enterprises.

Each year, organized retail theft is responsible for significant economic losses to retailers, which are then passed along to the American consumer. While it is difficult to pinpoint the exact annual dollar loss caused by this crime problem, retailers estimate all crimes where they are victims results in billions of dollars in losses.

The tax revenue losses attributable to ORT also negatively impact states. In the face of the current economic downturn, the hundreds of millions of dollars in revenue losses to our states can be considered catastrophic.

This crime problem also has the potential to negatively impact consumer health and safety. Specifically, the unsuspecting consumer faces potential health and safety risks from legitimate products which may have been mishandled by the criminal enterprises who stole them for resale to consumers. In many cases, stolen infant formula, pharmaceuticals, and other consumables are not stored under proper conditions. When these items are reintroduced into the retail market, they may pose a significant health risk to the consumer. The potential threat is perhaps most evident in cases in which infant formula is stolen, repackaged and then resold to both knowing and unknowing wholesalers, who then sell the infant formula to government food programs and discount stores. In addition to these concerns, the potential for intentional product tampering prior to the reintroduction of the stolen merchandise into the retail market is significant.

Also of concern for the FBI, in particular, is the potential nexus between organized retail theft syndicates and other criminal enterprises. In 2006, for example, nine members of an alleged Michigan smuggling operation were arrested, accused of taking part in a global scheme involving bootlegged cigarettes, phony Viagra and counterfeit tax stamps, and sending a cut of their illicit profits to Hezbollah.

The FBI has also investigated criminal ties between members of the international street gang MS-13 and fencing rings suspected of trafficking in millions of dollars in stolen medicine and other retail goods.

Challenges

There are many challenges on the road to combating organized retail theft. Lack of available resources to state and local police departments, who have the primary responsibility for investigating most retail crimes, is a huge hurdle. Sharing information between public and private enterprise is another.

As with other forms of criminal enterprise, there is a loose hierarchy within organized retail theft groups. Specifically, these groups utilize low-level 'boosters' – those who actually steal the merchandise and higher level 'fencers,' who frequently coordinate booster thefts. Often, these boosters are illegal immigrants working off a debt or individuals suffering from some form of addiction. If these low-level boosters are removed from the criminal enterprise, others will simply step in to take their place.

These criminal groups are also particularly nimble – able to easily change their appearance, alter their method of operation, and particularly adept at circumventing security devices and procedures. Groups typically utilize methods ranging in sophistication from the development and use of counterfeit receipts and UPC codes to refund and check/credit card fraud to something as basic as the 'grab and run.' They frequently identify store locations with Global Positioning Systems (GPS), identify escape routes, use false identification, utilize rented or borrowed vehicles, and employ diversionary tactics in stores. They are known to travel from state to state or city to city following interstate corridors around large cities.

Further, the wide reach of the Internet and online auction sites has provided global market places for entrepreneurs and, not surprisingly, criminal enterprises.

Law Enforcement/Private Industry Response

Sophisticated ORT groups can best be dismantled through a coordinated and cooperative effort between law enforcement and the retail industry. In December 2003, the FBI established an ORT Initiative to identify and disrupt multi-jurisdictional ORT groups, using federal statutes such as Conspiracy, Interstate Transportation of Stolen Property, and Money Laundering. Increased information sharing and cooperation between law enforcement and the private sector will enable both to gain a better understanding of the full nature and extent of the threat ORT poses, as well as to identify the best methods for law enforcement and the retail industry to attack this crime problem.

Additionally, Congress passed legislation signed by the President in January 2006 that required the Attorney General and the FBI, in consultation with the retail community – specifically, the National Retail Federation (NRF) and the Retail Industry Leader's Association (RILA) -- to build a system for information-sharing, to include intelligence as well as lessons learned and best practices regarding ORT. As you may already be aware, the result of that measure - the Law Enforcement Retail Partnership Network (LERPnet) - was subsequently launched in 2007.

The database, which is housed and run by the private sector, allows retail members to track and identify organized retail theft via a secure web portal. To date, nearly 100,000 retail locations are included in the data, which represents $1.17 trillion in retail sales or nearly 25% of all retail sales in one year.

With a recently signed Memorandum of Understanding (MOU), law enforcement will also be able to access LERPnet via the FBI's Law Enforcement Online to search reported incidents and track organized retail theft throughout the country. This partnership between law enforcement and private industry provides for greater efficiency in intelligence gathering and dissemination, enabling increased arrests, prosecutions, and recoveries of stolen merchandise.

Intelligence goes hand-in-hand with partnerships. One good piece of intelligence can be the breakthrough needed to make a vital connection or solve a case. By arming the retail industry with the infrastructure necessary to share such intelligence, it is our hope that they – along with their partners in law enforcement – are better able to thwart criminal efforts and reduce subsequent losses. Previously, individual retailers reported thefts to local law enforcement, but no uniform method of tracking these crimes across jurisdictions existed.

In addition to LERPnet and coordination with the retail industry, the FBI is identifying and targeting multi-jurisdictional ORT groups utilizing existing task force resources. Currently, there are seven FBI-led Major Theft Task Forces which are located in the Chicago, El Paso (2), Memphis, Miami (2) and New York Field Offices. Staffed by FBI Agents and other federal, state and local law enforcement officers, the task forces are responsible for conducting investigations in the major theft areas of ORT, cargo, vehicle, and jewelry theft crimes. Further, in cases where an organized retail theft enterprise can be tied to other criminal entities, additional FBI or law enforcement resources may be able to assist.

These task forces, which combine the resources of local, state and federal law enforcement, as well as retail loss prevention professionals, are applying investigative techniques and strategies which the FBI has successfully utilized to target traditional organized crime, including the development of a solid intelligence base and the use of undercover operations. Clearly, this approach increases the effectiveness and productivity of limited personnel and logistical resources, avoids the duplication of investigation resources, and expands the cooperation and communication among federal, state, and local law enforcement agencies as well as the retail industry.

SUCCESSES

The use of the task force approach to combating crime, coupled with successful partnerships within industry, is seen by the FBI as one of the most effective and efficient tools by which to identify, disrupt and dismantle any criminal enterprise. That strategy is working.

In February 2008, for example, seven individuals were indicted for participating in a scheme to shoplift merchandise and then sell it on the Internet auction site eBay. All seven defendants were charged with participating in a conspiracy to commit wire fraud and to engage in the interstate transportation of stolen property. That case was investigated by the FBI, Kansas City Police Department, and the Postal Inspection Service. It has since been prosecuted by the U.S. Attorney's Office, Western District of Missouri.

In May of that same year, 23 Organized Crime associates of the Gambino Crime Families – including a Gambino Crew Supervisor - were arrested based on a racketeering indictment charging them with operating an illegal enterprise involved in illegal gambling, extortion, fraud and labor racketeering. The fraud schemes pertained to eight or more associates involved in wire fraud because they created and used counterfeit UPC labels to obtain merchandise from numerous retail outlets. This six year investigation was conducted by the FBI as well as our partners at the U.S. Department of Labor, Office of Inspector General; the Internal Revenue Service; the New Jersey State Police; and, the Union County Prosecutors Office.

In August 2008, following months of investigation, the FBI and its law enforcement partners at the Internal Revenue Service, U.S. Immigration and Customs Enforcement, and the Broward County Sheriff's Department, participated in a raid of PharmaCare Health Services in Sunrise, Florida. The resulting indictments charged transportation of stolen goods, money laundering, conspiracy, and fraud. According to court documents, PharmaCare was actually a wholesaler that often purchased bulk quantities of mixed and damaged stolen products. Its employees were subsequently convicted of selling millions of dollars worth of over-the-counter medications, health and beauty aids that had been stolen from Walgreens, Target, CVS and Rite-Aid.

Chairman Scott, Ranking Member Gohmert and Members of the Subcommittee, I appreciate the opportunity to come before you today and share the work that the FBI is doing to address the problem posed by organized retail theft syndicates in this country. I am happy to answer any questions.

In: Organized Retail Crime
Editors: Blake H. Liventin

ISBN: 978-1-61122-768-0

Chapter 3

STATEMENT OF JANICE AYALA, ASSISTANT DIRECTOR FOR INVESTIGATIVE PROGRAMS, OFFICE OF INVESTIGATIONS, U.S. IMMIGRATION AND CUSTOMS ENFORCEMENT, DEPARTMENT OF HOMELAND SECURITY, BEFORE THE UNITED STATES HOUSE OF REPRESENTATIVES SUBCOMMITTEE ON CRIME, TERRORISM, AND HOMELAND SECURITY, HEARING ON "ORGANIZED RETAIL CRIME"

INTRODUCTION

Chairman Scott, Ranking Member Gohmert, and distinguished Members of the Subcommittee:

On behalf of Secretary Napolitano and Assistant Secretary Morton, I would like to thank you for the opportunity to testify today on the efforts of U.S. Immigration and Customs Enforcement (ICE) in the area of Organized Retail Crime (ORC). As you know, ICE is the largest investigative agency within the Department of Homeland Security. We protect national security and uphold public safety by targeting transnational criminal networks and terrorist organizations that seek to exploit vulnerabilities at our borders.

ICE investigates individuals and organizations that exploit vulnerabilities in financial systems for the purpose of laundering illicit proceeds. ICE also addresses the financial component of every cross-border criminal investigation. Naturally, this includes investigations into organized retail crimes. ICE's financial investigative authorities and unique capabilities specifically enable it to identify, dismantle, and disrupt the financial criminal enterprises that threaten our nation's economy and security. One of the most effective methods utilized to identify, dismantle, and disrupt organizations engaged in retail crime is to target the unlawful proceeds gained through their efforts.

ICE's Role in Battling Organized Retail Crime

ICE's Office of Investigations is well aware of the impact of organized retail crime on more than just our retail industry and economy. ICE investigations have demonstrated that profits generated from organized retail crime represent a clear threat to the U.S. financial sector because these profits may be laundered through U.S. and international financial systems. Similar to other criminal organizations, organized retail crime rings look for and exploit the vulnerabilities within these financial infrastructures to move and store their illicit proceeds.

ICE is involved in myriad investigations that target criminal activity including money laundering, narcotics trafficking, illegal importation and export, violation of intellectual property laws, human smuggling and trafficking, gang activity and human rights violations. ICE agents have broad investigative authorities under Titles 8, 18, and 31 of the United States Code, permitting them to pursue many different types of criminal violations, including complex banking and financial misconduct cases and seize assets of criminal enterprises engaged in immigration and customs violations. The melding of these authorities and unique capabilities given to, and used by, ICE enables it to identify, dismantle and disrupt the financial criminal enterprises that threaten our nation's economy and security.

From experience, ICE recognizes that organized retail crime groups engage in activities that cross over into one or more of ICE's ongoing initiatives or violate laws in which ICE has jurisdiction. ICE has been involved in a number of successful organized retail crime investigations over the past few years, but I would like to briefly discuss two of them.

Rosemont Wholesale, Inc.

ICE has been involved in the Rosemont Wholesale, Inc. investigation since 2005. At that time, ICE learned that individuals connected to Rosemont Wholesale, Inc. were possibly moving illicit proceeds abroad from the large-scale interstate sale of stolen retail products.

In 2005, retailers operating in the San Francisco Bay Area provided information to the Oakland Police Department regarding an ORC ring. Oakland Police Department subsequently forwarded that information to the ICE Special Agent in Charge (SAC) office in San Francisco.

ICE agents in San Francisco, with assistance from the Internal Revenue Service – Criminal Investigation (IRS-CI), the Oakland Police Department, the U.S. Department of Agriculture (USDA), and the Federal Bureau of Investigation (FBI), uncovered a ring involving thieves who stole over-the-counter products from large retailers throughout the San Francisco Bay Area. The stolen products were then resold through Rosemont Wholesale, Inc., a company involved in selling over-the-counter retail products such as medicines, razor blades, and baby formula, both over the Internet and throughout the San Francisco Bay Area to small, local grocery stores. Two fencing operations bought the stolen merchandise on behalf of Rosemont and generated illicit profits by selling it to Rosemont at a premium.

Rosemont then "laundered" the products, selling them through their online auction site and shipping them throughout the United States and Canada. Some of the proceeds from the criminal enterprise turned up in Yemen. In addition, Rosemont structured numerous banking transactions to avoid currency reporting requirements.

Following an extensive investigation, agents from ICE, IRS-CI, FBI, USDA, and officers from the Oakland Police Department executed search warrants at six locations in the San Francisco Bay Area. ICE seized more than 12 tractor-trailer loads of stolen merchandise valued at approximately $4.4 million. Charges were brought against eight defendants, including interstate transportation of stolen goods, securities, moneys, fraudulent state tax stamps or articles used in counterfeiting (18 U.S.C. § 2314), fraud and swindles (18 U.S.C. § 1341), laundering of monetary instruments (18 U.S.C. § 1956), structuring transactions to evade reporting requirements prohibited (31 U.S.C.

§ 5324), attempt to evade or defeat tax (26 U.S.C. § 7201), fraud and false statements (26 U.S.C. § 7206) and conspiracy to commit offense or to defraud the United States (18 U.S.C. § 371).

On October 16, 2009, Hassan Swaid, the President, Chief Executive Officer and owner of Rosemont Wholesale, Inc., was sentenced to 78 months in prison for his role in the conspiracy. Swaid was convicted on June 24, 2009, following a six-week jury trial. Five other members of this organization have pled guilty to various crimes, including structuring transactions to evade reporting requirements, conspiracy related to the interstate transportation of stolen goods, securities, moneys, fraudulent state tax stamps or articles used in counterfeiting, attempting to evade or defeat tax, and fraud and false statements. All remaining conspirators are currently awaiting sentencing.

Mohammed Ghali

ICE was involved in the Mohammed Ghali investigation after receiving information that a criminal organization he headed was involved in the interstate transportation of stolen merchandise and laundering the proceeds from the sale of this stolen merchandise internationally. According to sources ICE had developed, several members of the organization were also alleged to have direct ties to terrorist acts and/or organizations.

Mohammed Ghali was the leader of a criminal organization involved in large scale organized retail theft and international money laundering. Proceeds from Ghali's criminal activity were deposited in foreign financial institutions with weak anti-money laundering programs.

Members of the Ghali organization recruited hundreds of shoplifters and drug addicts to steal over-the-counter medicinal products, prescription drugs, and other specific items such as infant formula, glucose test strips, razors, and pregnancy test kits. These items were then repackaged and sold to wholesalers and retailers.

The organization used numerous convenience stores owned and operated by members of the organization in the Fort Worth, Texas area as fencing locations. Shoplifters and thieves utilized elaborate schemes to obtain the products such as counterfeit coupons, price matching schemes, and manufacturing counterfeit uniform price code labels. They also committed fraud through the use of food stamps and Women, Infant and Children Programs. In some instances, large quantities of products were obtained through armed robbery and warehouse thefts. For example, a shipment of

Viagra valued at over $1 million was stolen from a legitimate drug wholesaler, purchased by members of the Ghali organization, and then resold on the street.

To further expose the criminal organization, ICE initiated a joint undercover operation between its Dallas SAC office, the Fort Worth Police Department, and the Food and Drug Administration. The investigation utilized a number of investigative techniques, including the use of confidential informants, wiretaps, video and audio surveillance, undercover meetings and pen registers. Members of the loss prevention community also participated throughout the course of the investigation. Agents conducted approximately 93 undercover transactions in which property was specially marked, represented as stolen and sold to members of the organization. As a result of the investigation, approximately 35 members of the organization were charged with state and federal violations, including conspiracy, possession of stolen goods, interstate transportation of stolen property, receipt of stolen goods, and money laundering. Ghali, the leader of the organization, was convicted and sentenced to serve 14 years in federal prison. He also was ordered to forfeit two residences and $527,627 in cash that was seized during the investigation.

While I cannot discuss the specifics of ongoing organized retail crime investigations, ICE is currently working on active cases related to organized retail crime in Texas, Illinois, California and Florida.

Organized Retail Crime Pilot Program

ICE has become increasingly involved in investigations that target organized retail crime due to the interstate and international shipments of stolen goods and the corresponding movement of illicit proceeds from the sale of these stolen goods.

ICE has developed a pilot program to enhance the agency's ability to address the organized retail crime threat. The ORC Pilot Program was launched on July 6, 2009, in Houston, Los Angeles, Miami and New York, and is scheduled to last for an initial period of six months. The ORC Pilot Program focuses on four primary areas: 1) the development of a threat assessment to determine how these groups are engaged in crimes over which ICE has jurisdiction; 2) the development of a tracking system aimed at assessing ICE's involvement in ORC cases; 3) the development of a database that will be made available to the field with retail industry contacts for the affected ICE offices, which compliments the existing information contained in the National Retail Federation's LERPnet database by placing ICE agents in contact with members of the retail community throughout the country; and 4) an enhanced effort to explore fully how these groups are exploiting systemic vulnerabilities in the banking system to launder their profits.

The ORC Pilot Program, which is being funded with base investigative resources, encompasses all types of ORC-related criminal activities under the jurisdiction of ICE, including those committed over the Internet. Since the pilot program was launched just over four months ago, it is still too early to conduct an accurate analysis of its overall effectiveness. However, based on previous successful ICE investigations into organized retail crime, we have been able to develop some indicators of suspicious banking activity related to ORC. These indicators include:

- Business checks written to individuals, as opposed to legitimate suppliers.
- Business checks cashed at the banks from which the checks originated, instead of being deposited into another business' bank account.
- Business checks written to cash on a regular basis in amounts that exceed a business's petty cash requirement.
- Multiple checks written on the same day to cash to ensure the amount of each check does not exceed $10,000.
- Multiple money orders in increments of $500 or less deposited into bank accounts in which the remitter of the money order is the same as the authorized signers on the bank accounts for which the checks are being deposited.
- Subjects of questionable financial transactions maintaining the same address.
- Occupations listed for the subjects of questionable financial activities that are not commensurate to the volume and type of the financial activities.
- Checks drawn from the questionable financial activities that are negotiated in foreign countries.
- Cash deposits related to the questionable financial activities involving currency in $100 denominations.

Conclusion

While the organized retail crime initiative is only a pilot program at this time, based on our preliminary results of the threat assessment, ICE hopes to develop it into an ongoing initiative.

I would like to thank the Subcommittee for this opportunity to testify and for your continued support of ICE, DHS and our law enforcement mission. I will be happy to answer any questions that you may have at this time.

In: Organized Retail Crime
Editors: Blake H. Liventin

ISBN: 978-1-61122-768-0

Chapter 4

Statement of John R. Large, Special Agent in Charge, Criminal Investigative Division, Office of Investigations, U.S. Secret Service, before the House Committee on the Judiciary Subcommittee on Crime, Terrorism, and Homeland Security, Hearing on "Combating Organized Retail Crime: The Role of Federal Law Enforcement"

Good morning, Chairman Scott, Ranking Member Gohmert and distinguished members of the Subcommittee. Thank you for the opportunity to testify today on the investigative responsibilities of the United States Secret Service (Secret Service).

While the Secret Service is perhaps best known for protecting our nation's leaders, we were established in 1865 to investigate and prevent the counterfeiting of United States currency. As the original guardian of the nation's financial payment system, the Secret Service has a long history of protecting American consumers, industries, and financial institutions from fraud. Congress continues to recognize the Secret Service's 144 years of investigative expertise in financial crimes and over the last two decades has expanded our statutory authorities to include access device fraud (18 USC §1029), which includes credit and debit card fraud. Congress has also given the Secret Service concurrent jurisdiction with other law enforcement agencies for identity theft (18 USC §1028), computer fraud (18 USC §1030), and bank fraud (18 USC §1344). We take our mission to combat these crimes seriously and as a result, the Secret Service is recognized worldwide for its investigative expertise and innovative approaches to detecting, investigating, and preventing financial crimes.

To accomplish its investigative mission, the Secret Service operates 142 domestic offices (including domicile offices) and 22 foreign offices in 18 countries. The agency works closely with other federal, state, and local law enforcement, as well as other U.S. government agencies and foreign counterparts to maximize its efforts.

Financial Fraud and Electronic Crimes

In recent years, the combination of the information revolution and the effects of globalization have caused the investigative mission of the Secret Service to evolve. Through our work in the areas of financial and electronic crime, the Secret Service has developed particular expertise in the investigation of identity theft, false identification fraud, credit card fraud, debit card fraud, check fraud, bank fraud, and cyber crime, including computer intrusions. In Fiscal Year 2008, agents assigned to Secret Service offices across the United States arrested over 5,600 suspects for financial crimes violations. These suspects were responsible for approximately $442 million in actual fraud loss to individuals and financial institutions.

The Secret Service continues to observe a marked increase in the quality, quantity, and complexity of financial crimes, particularly offenses related to identity theft and access device fraud. Criminals often seek the personal identifiers generally required to obtain goods and services on credit, such as Social Security numbers, names, and dates of birth. Identity crimes also involve the theft or misuse of an individual's financial identifiers such as credit card numbers, bank account numbers, and personal identification numbers (PINs).

In the 1980s and 1990s, criminals obtained stolen personal and financial information through traditional means, such as theft of mail, theft of trash from businesses or victims, home and vehicle burglaries, and theft of a victim’s wallet or purse. While these low-tech methods of theft remain popular, criminal activity has also evolved so that criminals now employ newer, more high-tech methods for obtaining large quantities of stolen information.

Recent trends observed by law enforcement show that today's criminals continue to seek to compromise victims' personal and financial information through the use of computers and the Internet to launch cyber attacks targeting citizens and financial institutions. Cyber criminals have become adept at stealing victims' personal information through phishing emails, account takeovers, malicious software, hacking attacks, and network intrusions resulting in data breaches.

The Secret Service is particularly concerned about cases involving network intrusions of businesses that result in the compromise of credit and debit card numbers and all related personal information, and the subsequent exploitation of this data. A considerable portion of this type of electronic theft appears to be attributable to organized cyber groups, many of them based abroad, which pursue both the intrusions and the subsequent exploitation of the stolen data. Stolen credit card information is often trafficked in units that include more than just the card number and expiration date. These "full-info cards" include additional information, such as the card holder's full name and address, mother's maiden name, date of birth, Social Security number, a PIN, and other personal information that allows additional criminal exploitation of the affected individual.

Another rising trend is the increase in volume of trafficking "card track data" together with PINs. This data allows a criminal to manufacture a fully functional counterfeit credit or debit card and execute ATM withdrawals or other PIN-enabled transactions against an account.

The increasing level of collaboration among cyber-criminals raises both the complexity of investigating these cases and the level of potential harm to companies and individuals alike. Illicit Internet carding portals allow criminals to traffic stolen information in bulk quantities globally. These portals, or "carding websites," operate like online bazaars where criminals converge to trade in personal financial data and cyber-tools of the trade. The websites vary in size, from a few dozen members to some of the more popular sites boasting memberships of approximately 8,000 users. Within these portals, there are separate forums moderated by notorious members of the carding community. Members meet online and discuss specific topics of interest. Criminal purveyors buy, sell, and trade malicious software, spamming services, credit, debit, and ATM card data, personal identification data, bank account information, hacking services and other contraband.

In addition to the exploitation of credit and debit card accounts, many of the more sophisticated online criminal networks are now actively exploiting compromised online financial accounts. Criminals who gain access to victim accounts using online systems then execute fraudulent electronic banking transfers or sell the information to other criminals. The desire to exploit online bank accounts has led to the explosive growth of phishing scams, as well as the recent wave of malicious software, also known as "malware" or "crimeware," which is specifically designed to harvest account login information from the computers of infected victims. The technical sophistication of the illicit services readily available continues to grow. For example, the online fraud networks are increasingly leveraging the technical capabilities of "botnets" (i.e. networks of thousands of infected computers which can be controlled by a criminal from a central location) for financial attacks ranging in nature from the hosting of phishing and other malicious websites to the launching of widespread attacks against the online authentication systems of U.S. financial institutions.

The information revolution of the 1990s has turned our personal and financial information into a valuable commodity, whether it is being collected and brokered by a legitimate company or stolen by an identity thief. This information is no longer only an instrument used to facilitate a financial crime; it is now the primary target of criminals. Today, many companies have access to or store customer's personal financial information. This wealth of available personal information creates a target-rich environment for today's sophisticated criminals.

Globalization has made commerce easy and convenient for corporations and consumers – financial institutions and systems are readily accessible worldwide. Today's cyber-criminals have adapted to this new means of global trade and subsequently seek to exploit our dependence on information technology. With the explosion of Internet accessibility world-wide, criminals have modified their fraudulent schemes to a new, more anonymous and constantly evolving cyber arena. As a result, the Secret Service has modified its investigative techniques to keep pace with emerging technologies.

With this expansion of cyber crime, online auction houses have found themselves the victims or even the unwitting participants in organized criminal conspiracies. The Secret Service, while continuing to investigate financial crimes, has also opened criminal investigations into these organized cyber groups. The Secret Service has found these cases primarily evolve from access device fraud investigations, wherein, criminals who fraudulently purchase merchandise from traditional and online retailers and then resell the merchandise through online auction houses. In the recent past, the Secret Service, working closely with online auction houses, has successfully investigated and prosecuted several of these groups.

In May 2006, an internationally recognized telecommunications company contacted the Secret Service regarding the theft of approximately 20,000 cell phones from their plant in a major U.S. metropolitan area. The phones had left a warehouse in a shipment of five large pallets, and only two reached their final destination. The investigation led to employees of a nationally identified shipping company. The employees were interviewed regarding the missing shipments and eventually a manager of the shipping company confessed to running a stolen cell phone operation. The scheme involved cell phones that were sold to a re-seller at $75-$100 per phone, usually valued at $120-$150. Some of the phones were resold from a network of small collusive shops and some were sold at other venues, such as online auction houses. As a result of the investigation, the Secret Service recovered $1,549,000 of merchandise from a suspect's residence and all suspects in this case were arrested on federal charges for Aiding and Abetting, Conspiracy, and Access Device Fraud.

In October 2007, members of a Secret Service Electronic Crimes Task Force (ECTF), in cooperation with a District Attorney's Office, began an investigation into the criminal activities of an identified international currency transmittal service. The investigation revealed that suspects associated with this currency transmittal service recruited numerous individuals to sell fraudulently obtained merchandise over online auction houses. These proxy sellers advertised and took orders and/or bids for electronic merchandise at a significantly reduced price. Using stolen credit card information, the suspects purchased the ordered merchandise and then shipped it directly to the purchaser, or through another remailer. To date, the known fraud loss attributed to the group exceeds $4 million. Since the launch of the investigation, fourteen defendants have been arrested and are now in the United States and one defendant is currently in custody overseas awaiting extradition to the United States.

In March 2008, the Secret Service was contacted by a credit card issuing bank regarding credit cards that were compromised at a local restaurant. Subsequent investigation revealed four suspects were using "skimmed" credit card numbers to purchase gift cards from nationally identified retail stores. Upon obtaining the gift cards, the subjects would purchase electronic merchandise and sell those items and other gift cards through various online auction houses. All suspects associated with this case were subsequently arrested on federal charges for Access Device Fraud, Aggravated Identity Theft, and Conspiracy.

Fostering Partnerships and Combining Resources

Criminal groups involved in financial crimes routinely operate in a multi-jurisdictional environment. By working closely with other federal, state, and local law enforcement representatives, as well as foreign law enforcement, the Secret Service is able to provide a comprehensive network of information sharing, resource sharing, and technical expertise that bridges jurisdictional boundaries.

The Secret Service has established unique and vital partnerships with state, local, and other federal law enforcement agencies through years of collaboration on our investigative and protective endeavors. These partnerships enabled the Secret Service to establish a national network of Financial Crimes Task Forces (FCTFs) to combine the resources of the private sector and other law enforcement agencies in an organized effort to combat threats to our financial payment systems and critical infrastructures. The Secret Service currently maintains 37 FCTFs located in metropolitan regions across the country.

Further, in 1996, the Secret Service established the New York Electronic Crimes Task Force (ECTF) to combine the resources of academia, the private sector, and local, state and federal law enforcement agencies to combat computer-based threats to our financial payment systems and critical infrastructures. Congress has since directed the Secret Service in Public Law 107-56 to establish a nationwide network of ECTFs to "prevent, detect, and investigate various forms of electronic crimes, including potential terrorist attacks against critical infrastructure and financial payment systems."

To date, the Secret Service has established 28 ECTFs, including the first international ECTF based in Rome, Italy. Membership in our ECTFs include: 299 academic partners; over 2,100 international, federal, state and local law enforcement partners; and over 3,100 private sector partners. The Secret Service ECTF model is unique in that it is an international network with the capabilities to focus on regional issues. For example, the New York ECTF, based in the nation's largest banking center, focuses heavily on protecting our financial institutions and infrastructure, while the Houston ECTF works closely with partners such as ExxonMobil, Chevron, Shell, and Marathon Oil to protect the vital energy sector. By joining our ECTFs, all of our partners enjoy the resources, information, expertise, and advanced research provided by our international network of members while focusing on issues with significant regional impact.

Partnerships between law enforcement and the private sector are critical to the success of the ECTF's preventive approach. Our ECTFs collaborate with private sector technical experts in an effort to protect their system networks and critical information by encouraging the development of business continuity plans and routine risk management assessments of their electronic infrastructure. Greater ECTF liaison with the business community provides rapid access to law enforcement and vital technical expertise during incidents of malicious cyber crime. The ECTFs also focus on partnerships with academia to ensure that law enforcement is on the cutting edge of technology by leveraging the research and development capabilities of teaching institutions and technical colleges.

Another key element of success within the ECTF model is the Secret Service's Electronic Crimes Special Agent Program (ECSAP). This program is comprised of 1,148 Secret Service special agents who have received at least one of three levels of computer crimes-related training. These agents are deployed in more than 98 Secret Service offices throughout the world and have received extensive training in forensic identification, preservation and retrieval of electronically stored evidence. ECSAP agents are computer investigative specialists and among the most highly-trained experts in law enforcement, qualified to conduct examinations on all types of electronic evidence. This core cadre of special agents is equipped to investigate the continually evolving arena of electronic crime and have proven invaluable in the successful prosecution of criminal groups involved in computer fraud, bank fraud, identity theft, access device fraud, and various other electronic crimes targeting our financial institutions and private sector.

These resources allow ECTFs the potential to identify and address possible cyber vulnerabilities before criminals find and exploit them. This proactive approach has successfully prevented cyber attacks that otherwise would have resulted in large-scale financial losses to U.S. based companies or disruptions of critical infrastructures. The Secret Service task force model opens the lines of communication and encourages the exchange of information between all academic, private sector, and law enforcement partners.

Additionally, the National Computer Forensics Institute (NCFI) initiative is the result of a partnership between the Secret Service, the Department of Homeland Security (DHS), and the State of Alabama. The goal of this facility is to provide a national standard of training for a variety of electronic crimes investigations. The program offers state and local law enforcement officers, prosecutors, and judges the training necessary to conduct computer forensics examinations. Investigators are trained to respond to network intrusion incidents and conduct basic electronic crimes investigations.

Since opening on May 19, 2008, the Secret Service has provided critical training to 564 state and local law enforcement officials representing over 300 agencies from 49 states and two U.S. territories.

Community Outreach and Public Awareness

The Secret Service raises awareness of issues related to counterfeit, financial fraud, and electronic crimes, both in the law enforcement community and among the general public. The Secret Service has worked to educate consumers and provide training to law enforcement personnel through a variety of programs and initiatives. Agents from local field offices routinely provide community outreach seminars and public awareness training on the subjects of counterfeit currency, financial fraud, identity theft, and cyber crime. Agents often address these topics when speaking to school groups, civic organizations, and staff meetings involving businesses or financial institutions. In addition, the Secret Service provides training in the form of continuing education to state and local law enforcement. This training includes formal and informal classes which occur at field office sponsored seminars, police academies, and other various settings.

The Secret Service currently participates in a joint effort with the Department of Justice, the U.S. Postal Inspection Service, the Federal Trade Commission (FTC), the International Association of Chiefs of Police (IACP), and the American Association of Motor Vehicle Administrators to host identity crime training for law enforcement officers. In the last four years, Identity Crime Training Seminars have been held in over 18 cities nationwide, with two more expected by the end of the year. These training seminars are focused on providing local and state law enforcement officers with tools and resources that they can immediately put into use in their identity crime investigations.

In addition, the Secret Service is committed to providing our law enforcement partners with publications and guides to assist them in combating counterfeit activity, financial fraud and cyber crime. The Secret Service continues to collaborate with the Department of Treasury and the Bureau of

Engraving and Printing to produce and distribute various pamphlets, guides, posters, and visual aides pertaining to counterfeit currency detection.

Specific instructions pertaining to the seizure and analysis of electronic evidence should be provided to officers to ensure proper investigation and successful prosecution of cyber crime offenses. To provide this essential knowledge, the Secret Service published the "*Best Practices Guide for Seizing Electronic Evidence*." This pocket guide was designed for police officers and detectives acting as first responders and helps guide law enforcement officers in recognizing, protecting, seizing, and searching electronic devices in accordance with applicable statutes and policies.

The Secret Service also has collaborated with several of our law enforcement and corporate partners to produce the interactive, computer-based training programs known as "*Forward Edge*" and "*Forward Edge II*." The *Forward Edge* series is a CD-ROM that provides law enforcement and corporate investigators with practical training in order to recognize and seize electronic storage items.

Finally, the Secret Service produced an Identity Crime Video/CD-ROM, which contains over 50 investigative and victim assistance resources that local and state law enforcement officers can use when combating identity crime. This CD-ROM also contains a short identity crime video that can be shown to law enforcement which discusses why identity crime is important, what other departments are doing to combat identity crime, and what tools and resources are available. The Identity Crime CD-ROM is an interactive resource guide that was made in collaboration with the U.S. Postal Inspection Service, the FTC and the IACP.

CONCLUSION

As I have highlighted in my statement, the Secret Service is committed to our mission of protecting the integrity of U.S. currency and safeguarding the nation's critical financial infrastructure and financial payment systems. Although the Service's core responsibilities remain the same, our methods of investigation have changed to keep pace with emerging technologies. Through successful partnership with public and private task force members, the Secret Service continues to adapt to the ever evolving cyber criminal environment. The Secret Service dedicates significant resources to aggressively investigate all offenses within our purview to protect consumers and financial institutions.

This concludes my prepared statement. Thank you again for this opportunity to testify on behalf of the Secret Service. I will be pleased to answer any questions at this time.

In: Organized Retail Crime
Editors: Blake H. Liventin
ISBN: 978-1-61122-768-0

Chapter 5

Statement of Zane M. Hill, Deputy Chief Postal Inspector, National Headquarters, U.S. Postal Inspection Service, before the House Committee on the Judiciary Subcommittee on Crime, Terrorism and Homeland Security, Hearing on "Combating Organized Retail Crime: The Role of Federal Law Enforcement"

Mr. Chairman and members of the Committee: thank you for holding this hearing on organized retail crime. The Postal Inspection Service appreciates the opportunity to be here with our colleagues from the U.S. Secret Service, Federal Bureau of Investigation and Immigration and Customs Enforcement to talk about our efforts to thwart organized retail crime. The Postal Inspection Service is committed to protect the American public from criminals who use the United States Postal Service in furtherance of fraudulent schemes, including organized retail crime.

The Postal Inspection Service has a long, proud, and successful history of securing the nation's mail system and ensuring the public's trust in the mail. Postal Inspectors have been fighting consumer fraud since the mail fraud statute was enacted in 1872. The company name, address and "product" may change, but con artists take advantage of economic trends and current events to plan their schemes and illegal activities. With modern technology, the potential for the American public to be defrauded through the mail is much greater and potentially impacts more people than ever before.

Because it is essential the public have full trust and confidence in the mail, Postal Inspectors are intent on preserving the integrity of the U.S. Mail through vigorous law enforcement, public education, and crime prevention efforts.

Postal Inspectors are charged with ensuring the mails are safe and free from fraudulent schemes, illegal drugs, various forms of contraband, child pornography, as well as other dangerous products. Additionally, we work with other law enforcement and government agencies at the local, state, and federal level to ensure the Postal Service is not used to facilitate the commission of other crimes or as a conduit for the transportation of proceeds from illicit activities.

It is this commitment that makes the Postal Service the most trusted government agency and one of the most trusted organizations in the United States. It is the ongoing vigilance of the Postal Service and Postal Inspectors in identifying criminals who attempt to use the mails in furtherance of their illegal activities. The use of the mails in organized retail theft has not historically been one of the major types of criminal activities we have encountered. That being said, we are now aware of its potential impact and a number of these types of cases have been referred to us from other law enforcement agencies as well as the retail industry.

Our colleagues in federal, state, and local law enforcement, as well as corporate security professionals, are the principal investigators in the area of organized retail crime. When these crimes or aspects of these crimes cross or enter into the postal system, we have the jurisdiction and statutory authority to investigate and assist other law enforcement agencies and retailers in combating these illegal activities.

We generally see two types of schemes which I will discuss briefly: Internet auction fraud and Reshipper fraud. Both of these crimes take advantage of the increasing use of the on-line marketplace in order to sell the stolen or fraudulently obtained goods.

The Internet has become a critical component of the world's commerce. More and more businesses are increasing their use of this commerce channel. Likewise consumers have the convenience and ease of shopping in this expanded marketplace with a simple click of the mouse without having to leave home. This convenience though has a downside – criminals as well as others who seek to take advantage of consumers, now have a larger market in which to sell and distribute their stolen products while making substantial profits with fewer risks than the physical fencing operations that these criminals have historically used. By far, there is a greater reach for advertising of the ill-gotten products and the risk of detection is somewhat limited, making this online marketplace option so attractive to the organized retail crime groups.

As noted our jurisdiction in organized retail crime lies in the use of the mail in order to ship the stolen products or as a means to remit payment to the online seller. In these investigations, we have seen criminal groups utilize the full spectrum of postal products, including Priority Mail, Express Mail, postal money orders as well as Post Office boxes from which they run their fraudulent schemes.

One example of a recent Postal Inspection Service case began in early 2008. Postal Inspectors received a tip that owners of two Toledo, OH convienence stores were buying stolen merchandise, selling it on eBay and then shipping the items, both domestically and internationally via the Postal Service. Postal Inspectors determined that proceeds from the fraudulent sales were being laundered by the operators' relatives in Jordan. We alerted special agents of Immigration and Customs Enforcement (ICE) in July when it was determined one of the operators was leaving for Jordan on a flight from the Detroit Metro Airport, and was believed to be smuggling an unknown amount of cash. ICE special agents stopped the owner, his wife, and their two children at the airport and seized $75,000 in undeclared funds which were hidden in the children's clothing. The husband and wife each pled guilty to illegally smuggling cash and were sentenced to time in prison.

Postal Inspectors continued their investigation of the other suspect operator with excellent cooperation from eBay and PayPal and obtained records of the owner which identifed over 7,500 items valued at $650,000 that he had sold online. Postal Inspectors worked with loss-prevention specialists from the victim companies and identified most of the items as coming from their stores.

Throughout 2008, Postal Inspectors and corporate security investigators worked undercover, purchasing stolen items from online sites operated by the suspect. In February 2009, Postal Inspectors, ICE special agents, and Toledo, OH police executed a search warrant at the suspect's home and recovered boxes of stolen merchandise as well as maps of pharmacies he apparently planned to target in Cleveland, Columbus, and Toledo. He was arrested and charged with mail fraud. He pled guilty in August and is being detained until he is sentenced.

The second area of retail based crime we have become involved in is re-shipper fraud. In these types of cases, criminal organizations enlist individuals to receive and then reship products to other segments of the criminal enterprise generally to locations outside of the United States. In the majority of these cases, the products are obtained by retail crime groups through credit card theft as well as fraud. The re-shippers are oftentimes unwitting accomplices to the scheme, receiving and mailing the products based on instructions provided by the fraudsters. The re-shippers are then paid for their services. Many of these groups recruit the "re-shippers" in an attempt to further insulate themselves from detection, using a variety of ploys to trick individuals looking for easy work-at-home jobs. Ultimately, these re-shippers become part of the fraudulent activity. Retailers, legitimate shippers and financial institutions have all seen in increase in this type of crime. Again, the ability to move the stolen product with the least amount of exposure to those perpetrating the crimes is the reason for the use of the re-shipper approach.

As part of their operation recruiters for the groups post bogus job listings on the various Internet career sites purporting to employ "merchandising managers" and "package processing assistants." The employment is described as, "receiving packages in the mail and resending them to foreign addresses." This certainly sounds attractive as well as easy to the prospective participants. The groups further the scheme often providing bogus and fraudulently obtained postage-paid mailing labels to their re-shipper recruits. The Postal Service can also suffer significant losses as well as damage to its brand integrity when postal products or services are targeted by criminal schemes.

Re-shippers are also recruited by a variety of other fraudulent solicitations, such as on-line dating Web dating sites. In the typical "sweetheart scammer", the fraudster sends e-mails to the potential recruit in order get to know them. Once they have aroused their attention, the fraudster asks them to help the business or family by shipping packages to Europe or Africa.

Other scammers oftentimes claim to be working with a charity or mission which needs help getting "donated" merchandise delivered to third-world countries as well as other parts of the world.

In reality, both the "sweetheart" and the "charity worker" need assistance with smuggling goods out of the United States which were purchased with stolen and other fraudulently obtained credit cards. In the end there's no sweetheart or legitimate charity—even the mailing labels are either fraudulent or obtained using stolen credit cards.

The U.S. Postal Inspection Service continues to educate consumers about these fraudulent schemes using, for example, prevention-oriented messages delivered through online videos, newspaper and ad awareness campaigns (such as fakechecks.org), as well as via online publications, and our Web site at: www.usps.com/postalinspectors.

In closing, be assured the Postal Inspection Service remains committed to collaborating with our law enforcement and corporate partners to deal with the problem of distribution of illicit goods through on-line market places and ultimately the U.S. mail.

In: Organized Retail Crime
Editors: Blake H. Liventin

ISBN: 978-1-61122-768-0

Chapter 6

Testimony of Brade Brekke, Vice President, Assets Protection, Target Corporation, before the House Judiciary Subcommittee on Crime, Terrorism and Homeland Security, Hearing on "Organized Retail Theft: Fostering a Comprehensive Public-Private Response"

Introduction

I am pleased to provide written testimony on behalf of Target and to represent the Coalition Against Organized Retail Crime.

By way of background, the Coalition Against Organized Retail Crime, which has been together now for six years, is comprised of national manufacturing and retail organizations as well as individual companies from both sectors. In total, there are 32 members. A roster of all Coalition members can be found at the end of this written testimony. We are also pleased to recognize the formal support of the International Association of Chiefs of Police (IACP) in our effort to control retail crime and the Internet fencing of stolen property.

The Coalition wishes to commend Chairman Scott and Ranking Member Forbes for scheduling today's hearing. This new focus on this issue is a very timely and appropriate response to the problem of Organized Retail Crime that is victimizing practically every segment of the retail community from supermarkets and retail drug stores, to mass merchandisers, department stores, specialty shops, boutiques, and convenience stores among others. We commend the Chairman, Ranking Member, and this Committee for recognizing the runaway problem of organized retail crime (ORC) and its causes.

I would like to discuss three important issues concerning this problem:

- First, I will briefly describe the nature of retail crime today and how it has evolved;
- Second, I would like to describe our substantial efforts to combat retail crime and explain how the Internet fuels its dramatic growth.
- Finally, I will explain how we can join together in encouraging on-line auctions sites to help protect our communities by preventing their sites from becoming markets for stolen goods and without expending valuable criminal justice resources on more arrests and prosecutions.

Background on ORC

First of all, when I refer to Organized Retail Crime, I do not intend to discuss the different phenomenon of what is commonly referred to as "shoplifting." Obviously, this type of theft is well understood and within the experience of most retailers. Organized retail crime, however, refers to the growing problem of mostly gangs but sometimes individuals who are engaging in illegally obtaining retail merchandise through both theft and fraud in substantial quantities and as part of a commercial enterprise in which the merchandise is resold through large scale distribution networks. The tactics can vary from multi-person diversionary efforts, to abuse of emergency exit doors and employing counter measures such as foil lined bags to defeat electronic merchandise protection tags. These criminal commercial enterprises are of a different nature and a different scale from what we have come to understand as "shoplifting." As I will explain, the size of these enterprises is often a function of their ability to redistribute their stolen merchandise. And the Internet has transformed their ability to resell their stolen goods.

Yesterday, a for-profit retail theft may have focused on high-value individual items such as a watch or electronics that might garner economic return to the thief even if they had to sell it at a heavy discount. Today, commercial ORC gangs exhibit modern practices of inventory management to help them meet the growing demand for the entire range of stolen merchandise such as consumer electronics, heartburn medication, Dyson vacuum cleaners, printer cartridges, razors, DVDs, dental white strips, anti-histamines, over-the-counter painkillers, diabetes test kits, and increasingly, baby formula. The inclusion of baby formula is troubling since there is little likelihood that attention is paid to whether it is safely stored prior to resale.

Another interesting development is that some organized property rings actually use advanced "just-in-time" inventory control systems in which they first accept orders for goods and only then do they make up "shopping lists" that they direct their boosters to go out and steal.

These commercial rings are a growing problem throughout the United States affecting many sectors of the retail community from supermarkets and chain drug stores to mass merchandisers and specialty stores. Precise measurements of the true scope of this problem are impossible due to the inherently secretive nature of what is, after all, a criminal enterprise. Not surprisingly, criminal gangs do not publicly report either their sales or their thefts. Studies by different academics estimate the scope of the problem at different levels but consistently in the billions of dollars annually. The Federal Bureau of Investigation (FBI) interstate task force recently estimated that Organized Retail Crime accounted for up to $30 billion in losses annually at the store level. By any measure, it is a significant issue affecting our communities.

Retail Industry Efforts

For years, the retailing industry has vigorously worked to control organized retail crime and other forms of retail theft. According to industry studies, retailers collectively spend an estimated $12 billion annually to combat retail theft. These efforts include but are not limited to the following:

- new technologies in tamper resistant packaging,
- labeling technologies,
- merchandise protection fixtures,
- high tech surveillance camera with sophisticated computer analytics and remote monitoring,

- sophisticated background investigations for employees to identify ORC ring members,
- many thousands of dedicated loss prevention professionals and investigators,
- we at Target have even invested millions in establishing forensic laboratories with latent fingerprint and other capabilities that support not only our own ORC investigations but also other law enforcement prosecutions all at no charge to law enforcement.

Any suggestions that retailers are reducing their efforts to fight retail theft are erroneously misconstruing data by narrowing focusing on loss prevention staffing only. These estimates fail to consider the expenditures against retail theft that are part of our construction, human resources and information technology budgets. This is an enormously important and expensive effort for the retail industry. There is no question that these efforts will continue and grow. However, the continuing growth of retail crime and the damage it causes to communities must cause us all to recognize that something needs to be done to control the resale market for stolen goods.

E-Fencing

As has been recently reported in network news stories reported by both CNN and CNBC, (see attached) the explosive growth in retail crime has been fueled by the advent of technology in general and the Internet specifically.

Before the internet, the market for stolen goods was limited by several critical factors:

- First, buyers and sellers of stolen goods had to physically interact with one another face-to-face and this naturally limited the overall size of the market for stolen goods;
- Second, the face-to-face nature of stolen goods market meant buyers could usually recognize the questionable legality of the merchandise offered and were willing to pay much less for goods (generally in the range of $.30 on the dollar); this made profits lower;
- Finally, the personal nature of the stolen goods market, along with state and local pawnshop regulations, meant that sellers of stolen

goods had to *identify themselves and identify their goods with serial numbers.*

In the "bricks and mortar" world, it was difficult to operate with anonymity.

Today, that has all changed. The Internet has created a world wide market for stolen goods in which the sellers are anonymous and there is an enormous universe of buyers who are generally unaware of the nature of the goods sold. These unwitting buyers are usually willing to pay twice (close to $0.70 on the dollar) that which was previously available to fences in the "bricks and mortar" world.

Moreover, Internet fences are routinely evading the traditional laws used by state and local governments to protect our communities by controlling sales of stolen property.

Virtually all state and local pawnshop regulations require sellers to identify themselves and identify the serial numbers of goods sold. But on the Internet, there are currently no controls. This means that there are no limits on fences operating in the Internet and no assurances that the property consumers are buying is not stolen.

Not surprisingly, the enormous new profits available to organized retail crime rings are resulting in more and more boosters in the stores.

Proposed Requirements for Online Auction Companies

Retailers, in partnership with law enforcement, will continue to fight this problem. But the growth in organized retail crime - fueled by technology and Internet fencing - has reached such a scale that retail and law enforcement cannot successfully fight this problem one booster and one fence at a time.

Consideration of two statistics can put in perspective the scale of this problem relative to available criminal justice resources.

- In the most recent year, Target alone made approximately 75,000 theft apprehensions in its stores.
- By comparison, the total number of criminal cases in all federal district courts across the country is usually less than 60,000 cases in any one year.

What this means is that even if all of the U.S. Attorneys across the country stopped prosecuting bank robberies, fraud, drug trafficking and even terrorism, there still would not be enough capacity to prosecute even the apprehensions made by Target. Obviously, the entire industry makes hundreds of thousands of apprehensions annually. But sending even more people into the criminal justice system is not the answer and not what we are proposing. This also explains why cooperation from the Internet auction industry in individual cases and only when requested by law enforcement is also insufficient. We need to change behavior and the internet auction sites need to join us in this effort.

It was once said by some insightful observer that: "If the only tool you have is a hammer, then all of your problems begin to look like nails." Mr. Chairman, we can't keep addressing this issue by investigating and apprehending one fence at a time; we need to add a new approach to this problem.

Mr. Chairman, we need to have responsible internet auction sites make modest changes to their sites to help reduce sales of stolen property in the first place. And we can do this by applying traditional models of stolen property regulation to the Internet and inject some needed transparency to these transactions.

And, Mr. Chairman, transparency works. It is already being effectively used on other parts of the Internet. Today, every vehicle listed for sale on eBay Motors is accompanied by a Vehicle Identification Number (VIN) [the VIN itself can be verified for accuracy through Carfax] which permits ready and automated identification of any stolen car posted for sale. This requirement of posting identifying information has virtually eliminated the sale of stolen vehicles through this service. It could have the same effect in preventing sales of stolen iPods and vacuum cleaners.

Opponents to this proposal frequently cite alleged privacy concerns to oppose these requirements but the United Kingdom has employed a similar requirement for high volume Internet sellers for years without adverse consequences. Moreover, our suggestion is to limit the required identification of sellers to only the high dollar volume sellers. This will protect the privacy of infrequent sellers while preventing high volume commercial sellers from hiding in unnecessary anonymity.

These requirements are not unorthodox. As I mentioned earlier, these requirements, identification of sellers and providing serial numbers, are the very same features that are common in almost all state and local pawnshop laws. These simple requirements have been used by virtually all communities to protect themselves from property crime problems. These are the same requirements that sellers are evading by going on-line. This means that the advent of e-fencing has taken this traditional state and local issue and made it impossible for local law enforcement to control. Every local fencing operation with access to the Internet can now operate internationally and beyond the reach of local law enforcement. A federal solution is necessary to protect our communities.

We believe that law enforcement needs new tools to prosecute irresponsible internet auction sites and marketplaces that refuse to exercise due diligence over persons using their facilities. In this regard, what we are suggesting is that Internet auction sites who fail to exercise due diligence to prevent the facilitation of stolen property sales should be treated not unlike financial institutions that fail to exercise due diligence to identify and prevent money laundering by their customers.

RETAILERS WANT TO PARTNER WITH INTERNET AUCTION SITES

I want to make clear that we are not seeking the criminal prosecution of responsible Internet auction sites. Rather, we want to encourage them to join us in protecting our communities. In fact, we would expect that responsible Internet auction sites and their customers would welcome this opportunity to reduce the sale of stolen property online.

Retailers have already formed critical partnerships that will pay important dividends under the proposed legislation, if passed. For example, certain Coalition members, such the National Retail Federation (NRF), the Retail Industry Leaders Association (RILA) and the Food Marketing Institute (FMI) have recently partnered with the Federal Bureau of Investigations (FBI) to create a national data base, the Law Enforcement Retail Partnership Network (LRPNet) that tracks where ORC crimes are being committed throughout the country. This same database could be used to house and match the serial numbers of stolen merchandise to the serial numbers posted by online auctions sites. The partnership with the FBI could also be relied upon to ensure that the serial numbers and this database are used only to control criminal conduct and not misused for other purposes.

Conclusion

While retailers will continue to invest billions in trying to prevent organized retail crime and apprehend and prosecute the perpetrators, it is clear that the problem can not be solved by fighting these cases one by one and only in the shopping aisles. At the rate the Internet is growing and the constantly and rapidly escalating scale at which any criminal is now able to operate, it is clear that there is an immediate need to update the law to cover these 21st century criminal operations.

We can do this by applying proven methods such as transparency and the posting of serial numbers that permit the tracing of stolen property. These modest measures have already been proven to be effective, even in the Internet age. And these measures can reduce property crime without more arrests and incarceration.

Coalition against Organized Retail Crime

- Abbott Laboratories
- Ahold USA, Inc.
- Consumer Healthcare Products Association
- Cosmetic, Toiletry, and Fragrance Association
- CVS/pharmacy
- Duane Reade
- Eastman Kodak Company
- Eckerd Corporation
- Food Lion, LLC
- Food Marketing Institute
- Giant Food LLC
- Giant Food Stores LLC
- GlaxoSmithKline
- Grocery Manufacturers/Food Products Association
- International Formula Council
- National Association of Chain Drug Stores
- National Association of Convenience Stores
- National Community Pharmacists Association
- National Retail Federation
- Nestle

- Publix Super Markets, Inc.
- Retail Alliance
- Retail Industry Leaders Association
- Rite Aid Corporation
- Safeway Inc.
- Security Industry Association
- The Stop & Shop Supermarket Company
- Target Corporation
- Tops Markets, LLC
- Wal-Mart Stores, Inc.
- Walgreen Co.

In: Organized Retail Crime
Editors: Blake H. Liventin
ISBN: 978-1-61122-768-0

Chapter 7

WRITTEN TESTIMONY OF MR. ROBERT CHESNUT, SENIOR VICE PRESIDENT, RULES, TRUST AND SAFETY, EBAY INC., BEFORE THE HOUSE SUBCOMMITTEE ON CRIME, TERRORISM AND HOMELAND SECURITY, HEARING ON "ORGANIZED RETAIL THEFT PREVENTION: FOSTERING A COMPREHENSIVE PUBLIC-PRIVATE RESPONSE"

Mr. Chairman, Ranking Member Forbes and members of the Committee, My name is Robert Chesnut, and I am the Senior Vice President for Rules, Trust and Safety for eBay Inc. I would like to thank the committee for giving eBay this opportunity to discuss the importance of fostering real and effective solutions to the problem of Organized Retail Crime, and I ask that my full statement be entered into the committee record.

Prior to joining eBay in 1999, I was an Assistant United States Attorney in the Eastern District of Virginia for 11 years. For 5 of those years I served as Chief of the Major Crimes Unit. My career at eBay has been focused on keeping our site safe for our community by working with the law enforcement community, the private sector, policymakers, consumer protection agencies and state and federal legislatures, so I very much appreciate the opportunity to speak with you today on behalf of eBay about this important topic.

eBay recognizes that organized retail theft is a serious problem facing many retailers in this country. This Committee should be applauded for the commitment it has shown to addressing this problem, compiling clear evidence that this is a problem that stretches back many years and occurs at a disturbingly large scale. We believe that it is a problem that deserves serious attention by lawmakers, law enforcement and all aspects of the retail businesses impacted. eBay stands ready to work with all stakeholders on balanced and thoughtful responses, including responses that account for the internet as one among many and varied ways that criminals attempt to sell stolen goods to unsuspecting consumers.

Let me be clear, eBay takes the problem of stolen goods, and all forms of illegal activity that can impact our users, very seriously. We have the most pro-active policies and tools to combat fraud and illegal activity of all the major internet commerce companies. There are over 2000 eBay Inc. employees around the world working to combat all forms of on-line fraud, including the sale of stolen goods. As we have grown as a business over the last 12 years, we have dedicated more and more resources to the fight against criminal activity that harms our users.

When eBay first emerged as a dynamic way for people to buy and sell items online back in 1995, there were really no rules in place for our users to follow. We established the feedback system which gave each member a rating for each transaction that any user could see, and for the most part all of the trust between buyers and sellers was based on that system in the early years of eBay. But the company realized in those early years that in order to become a truly safe and trusted e-commerce site we needed to put policies and tools in place to make sure that illegal items and harmful sellers were quickly identified and removed from our platform. We created clear policies about what is allowed and not allowed to be listed on the site and built state-of-the art tools to enforce those policies. We developed advanced anti-fraud tools to identify suspicious behavior, remove members who engaged in harmful practices and take steps to keep them from coming back on the site. And we established a global Fraud Investigations Team to partner with law enforcement to make sure that criminals who seek to abuse our community of users get prosecuted to the fullest extent of the law. Largely as a result of these efforts, we now have trading platforms in 38 countries with over 240 million registered users. At any one time around 100 million items are listed for sale on eBay around the world. Millions of transactions take place everyday on eBay where both the buyer and seller walk away totally satisfied. Here in the United States, over 750,000 Americans make all or a large percentage of their income selling items on eBay.

Our acquisition of the online payment provider PayPal in 2002 only enhanced our ability to keep our users safe. PayPal offers our members a safe way to pay online, and in the last 5 years we have merged PayPal's anti-fraud experts with the engineers, statisticians and fraud modelists at eBay to create an industry-leading team of experts dedicated to keeping our sites and our community of users secure and safe. We dedicate significant resources toward cooperating with law enforcement agencies around the world. I am one of 8 former law enforcement officials that work at eBay and PayPal, and the fact that we have a fairly large internal contingent of folks from that community helps us understand the challenges faced by enforcement agencies and how we can help those folks do their jobs and keep our users safe.

Our Fraud Investigations Team works closely with law enforcement officials at the federal, state and local levels, and we have teams in San Jose and Salt Lake City to serve enforcement agencies throughout North America. Because we operate a truly global marketplace, we also have Fraud Investigation Teams in Dublin, Ireland and Dreilinden, Germany to serve law enforcement in Europe and Asia. Earlier this week, two of our law enforcement liaisons were in Romania working with officials there to combat fraudulent activity based in that country. This is the 6th time that our US-based staff has traveled to Romania in the last three years, and we have an attorney based in Eastern Europe who is dedicated full-time to working with police and prosecutors in that region. We make it easy for law enforcement officials to find us--we have dedicated hotlines, fax numbers and email addresses for law enforcement to be able to reach us quickly and efficiently. When agencies request records from us to support their enforcement actions, they receive those records in days---not weeks or months, as can be the case with other companies.

In addition to providing the records necessary to bring cases, our Fraud Investigations Team trains law enforcement officials around the United States and globally on the best way to combat crime online. My colleagues and I have spent a lot of time on the road in the last several years building relationships with enforcement agencies and teaching them how to investigate eBay and PayPal cases. In 2006 alone, we trained over 3000 law enforcement personnel in North America about online fraud in the eBay/PayPal context and how we can help them prosecute criminals who attempt to abuse our users. The assistance that our teams provide to law enforcement agencies around the world lead to an average of two arrests every single day. Our Fraud Investigations has worked on numerous cases with both law enforcement and loss prevention staff from the large retailers to make sure that thieves get prosecuted.

Our policies and commitment to combating the sale of stolen goods on eBay are straightforward. eBay is no place for the sale of stolen goods, and the transparency of our site combined with our commitment to working with law enforcement makes it an unwelcome venue for "fencing." The reality is that eBay is the riskiest way for a criminal to try to sell stolen products over the internet. We work both reactively and proactively with law enforcement, often referring cases out to the appropriate agency where we detect fraudulent behavior by one of our sellers, including the listing of stolen goods. When any retailer has concrete evidence to the effect that stolen property is on our site, we will work with them and law enforcement to address the problem, including sharing information about a targeted seller with the appropriate enforcement agency. This process already exists and we believe it works well.

In addition to our work with the law enforcement community, we have been engaging the retail industry for many years now to strengthen our relationships with retailer trade associations as well as individual companies to find ways we can work together to combat the sale of stolen property on eBay. We have held meetings with retailers all over the U.S. to hear their concerns and to explain how we can work with them on these issues. We have provided training to loss prevention teams about how to use the eBay website to investigate suspicious listings and gather information that can be used to bring a case to law enforcement. The manager of our Fraud Investigation Team in San Jose is presenting today at a joint law enforcement/retailer conference on Organized Retail Theft in Seattle, where over 400 officials from the retailer loss prevention community will be in attendance along with folks from local, state and federal law enforcement communities.

In addition to our outreach to the law enforcement and retailer communities, we have also taken additional steps internally over the last year to keep bad sellers off of eBay before they have a chance to harm our buyers. All new sellers on eBay.com must register a credit card with us and they must accept PayPal as a payment option. By requiring new sellers to take these steps we lower the chances of a criminal attempting to use our trading platform to commit fraud, as criminals don't generally like to provide financial information and use payment systems that make it easy to track them down once their illegal behavior becomes apparent. We have revamped our feedback system to allow buyers to provide much more detailed ratings of a seller's transactional performance. We have put higher standards in place for seller performance and suspend sellers who to a significant extent fail to satisfy their buyers. Sellers who fail to deliver the goods at all get referred out to law enforcement for prosecution. Let me reiterate that the delivery of stolen goods, counterfeit goods, or no goods at all is a horrible buyer experience for our customers. In the relatively rare circumstances where these activities take place, the buyer generally leaves our site and never comes back. And probably tells everyone he or she knows to never buy anything on eBay. Fighting fraud and keeping bad sellers off of our site are vital to our success as a business.

Regarding the broader ORC problem, this Committee has done significant work developing a record of this troubling issue. In terms of the distribution of stolen goods, your March 2005 Committee Report lists the following major venues: small shops (including beauty shops, gas stations, music stores, bars and gyms), flea markets, pawn shops, local fences, truck stops, newspaper ads, overseas buyers, and yes, the Internet through all types of web sites and chat forums. The Committee report also described how unscrupulous middlemen sell significant volumes of stolen goods back to traditional retailers blended in with legitimate products.

My point in mentioning the breadth of the process of turning stolen goods into money is that there are many avenues for this illicit process. Most of them are decidedly low tech in nature. While some tech savvy criminals are finding ways to use internet technologies, sensible solutions should address the entire range of distribution methods and not place disproportionate focus on less popular methods. Many large manufacturers and retailers have a negative view of the eBay marketplace because we provide an incredibly efficient secondary market for their goods. Our sellers are perceived by some as their competition, and one way to attack efficient secondary market competitors that sell goods at low prices is to suggest that there is something shady about those sales, when in reality those sales are completely legitimate.

This past summer there was a story in USA Today about the disdain that many large retailers have for individual entrepreneurs who use the Internet, usually eBay, to resell their products. A spokesperson from Gymboree, the popular children's clothing chain, explained their 5-item-per-customer limit by stating that "we need to protect our image…we don't want people to think we're selling things on eBay." A colleague of mine at eBay sells her kids' Gymboree clothes on eBay once they grow out of them. Those clothes are then worn by the buyer's kids, and my colleague uses the money to buy new clothes for her growing children. This is a truly efficient use of consumer goods, but Gymboree does not like it, as they seem to feel that the only place you should be able to buy Gymboree clothes is at the Gymboree store.

One approach to a legislative solution to the problem of organized retail theft is simple: increase the criminal penalties for this conduct. If these crimes are currently classified as misdemeanors, upgrade them to felonies. If the jail sentences tied to these crimes are too short, lengthen them. We have supported legislation in a number of states calling for tougher penalties, mandatory sentences and higher priority prosecutions of these criminals. We would support the same at the federal level. These steps will make these cases more attractive to law enforcement and will make judges more likely to put these criminals in jail rather than giving them probation. If these thieves make the unwise choice to use eBay to try and sell their stolen goods, we don't just want them off of eBay, we want them to see the inside of jail cell.

eBay has always been committed to providing a safe, well-lit marketplace. We believe that this commitment to our community has been key to growing eBay into the world's largest global online marketplace. Working in a cooperative relationship with business partners and law enforcement has been central to this effort, and we will continue in that manner going forward.

We look forward to working with this Committee on ways to effectively empower law enforcement to fight the problem of Organized Retail Crime. We stand ready to do our part to combat the long-term problem of retail theft in a balanced and responsible way. We believe that law enforcement is crucial to solutions regarding illegal activity, and we believe it is crucial across the board to protect the privacy and rights of the law-abiding citizens and small business people.

In: Organized Retail Crime
Editors: Blake H. Liventin

ISBN: 978-1-61122-768-0

Chapter 8

Testimony of Karl Langhorst, Director, Loss Prevention, Randall's/Tom Thumb a Safeway Company, before the House Judiciary Subcommittee on Crime, Terrorism and Homeland Security, Hearing on "Organized Retail Theft: Fostering a Comprehensive Public-Private Response"

Chairman Conyers, Chairman Scott, Congressmen Smith and Forbes, and members of the committee, good morning. Thank you for the opportunity to testify before the Crime Subcommittee today on the growing problem of organized retail crime. My name is Karl Langhorst, Director of Loss Prevention for Randall's/Tom Thumb of Texas, a Safeway company. Safeway Inc. is a Fortune 100 company and one of the largest food and drug retailers in North America. The company operates 1,755 stores in the United States and western Canada and had annual sales of $40.2 billion in 2006.

I have been invited here to share with you our experience with the increasing problem of organized retail crime (ORC). Retailers have always had to deal with shoplifting as part of doing business, but let me be clear, ORC is not shoplifting. It is theft committed by professionals, in large volume, for resale. It is being committed against retailers of every type at an increasing rate. Safeway estimates a loss of $100 million dollars annually due to ORC. According to the FBI, the national estimate is between $15-30 billion annually.

Let me describe for you how sophisticated and organized these enterprises are. In a typical scenario that repeats itself hundreds of times each day, teams of boosters, or hired thieves, come into the store with a shopping list of desired product provided by the fence – the person behind the organization. Typical items stolen from Safeway stores include over the counter medicines such as Prilosec, Tylenol, and Abreva, razor blades, Crest White Strips, Oil of Olay and other beauty products, diabetic test strips, and baby formula. Using well coordinated efforts and highly sophisticated methods to elude store security and law enforcement, they sweep the shelves clean of hundreds of dollars of product at a time. They are in and out within a matter of 3 to 4 minutes. They often leave undetected and move on to other stores. Typically, boosters will hit 10 to 15 retailers a day, in many areas criss-crossing state lines and jurisdictions, before going back to the fence to get payment for the goods they have stolen and to receive their marching orders for the next day. Their payment usually amounts to about twenty cents on the dollar. The fence then sells the items at traditional brick and mortar stores, flea markets, or - increasingly – online. They have great incentives to sell online because they know that they can operate anonymously and are protected, they can move more merchandise more quickly and to a broader audience, and they can receive the highest return for items sold online.

You may ask what Safeway is doing to prevent ORC at the store level – why don't we just hire a few more guards? The simple answer is that guards posted at store entrances provide only so much protection. In addition, Safeway has taken a step unprecedented in the grocery industry, of creating a whole division to combat ORC, employing special investigators across the US and Canada. This is in addition to the loss prevention teams based in each of our divisions. Because of the prevalence of ORC in our stores, special teams of ORC undercover agents have been trained and deployed into the stores. These agents understand the difference in detecting and apprehending the boosters versus simple shoplifters. Additionally, store personnel are trained and spend significant time in the store performing additional steps to prevent ORC at store level. There are special markings on high theft items to help deter theft. We limit quantities of this merchandise on the shelf to try and minimize losses, and we have invested in specialized shelving and display fixtures to thwart theft within the store. Unfortunately, these measures also make it difficult for customers to shop as easily as we would like and severely restricts the sale of these items. Safeway has implemented additional layers of security throughout the supply chain – from warehouse, to the loading dock, to the shelves. We have spent a tremendous amount of money in training and awareness campaigns among other retailers and law enforcement. Further, state of the art digital camera systems are installed in all of our stores at a cost of millions of dollars in order to aid law enforcement and our own investigators and store management teams in identifying the boosters who repeatedly steal from our stores.

In spite of our extraordinary efforts, our company continues to see a steady increase of our health, beauty and cosmetic goods sold on the internet in high volume and offered below cost of what retailers can obtain it directly from the manufacturer. Fences have quickly learned that the anonymity of the internet presents an extremely low risk way to sell stolen goods and are abandoning the previous model of brick and mortar locations and flea markets that were once used to dispose of this type product. Online marketplaces such as eBay are being used as internet pawn shops, and are largely unregulated.

We have has some successes in fighting ORC. In 2001 the Portland division of Safeway opened an investigation of three major fences and presented the information to the FBI. Over the course of the next three years Safeway and the FBI continued the investigation and successfully broke up a multistate ORC network operating from Oregon to Texas to Florida that ultimately resulted in the seizure of over $3 million in product, $950,000 in cash and federal criminal prosecution of 49 suspects. The suspects told federal investigators that they resold much of the stolen product on eBay because of the anonymity assured by the site.

Last year, in cooperation with Walgreens, Wal Mart and other retailers, our Northern California division worked a case with ICE agents that resulted in the seizure of product valued at $5 million dollars and the arrest and prosecution of Yemeni nationals. These individuals operated a warehouse containing 12 tractor trailers full of merchandise - 850,000 pieces of HBC product, as well as a website for internet sales.

Just this week, state agents in Texas and Safeway ORC investigators completed an over year long investigation and shut down a long time fence that was taking in an estimated 4 million dollars in stolen HBC product and who employed over 100 boosters. The fence was selling to another individual who was marketing it over the internet on both his own web site and eBay. In this case, many of the boosters were known drug users and the stolen product was stored under conditions that were not approved for these items. Storing these items in unregulated conditions can render the products ineffective, or in the worst case actually harm unsuspecting consumers, as in the case of baby formula.

In each of these cases, we could have had quicker, more thorough investigations and clearer rules under which the suspects could be prosecuted if we had a federal law in place specifically to address ORC. Federal law enforcement and prosecutors are interested in prosecuting ORC cases, but they lack the tools and resources necessary to bring these cases to bear. Investigation of these types of cases is extremely difficult. A federal ORC bill would establish a definition of ORC in statute, help eliminate the state to state jurisdictional cherry picking by thieves, and would be especially helpful in making efencing a less attractive option for criminals to sell stolen property. Operators of sites such as eBay have historically failed to provide any meaningful information to retail investigators. Without this cooperation, we are severely hampered in securing the evidence needed by federal investigators to even open an investigation.

The need for a federal solution to address the current "free for all" of electronic fencing is obvious. The information we are seeking from online marketplaces is no more cumbersome than is currently in place for brick and mortar providers of the same type operations. In many states sellers of product such as HBC must have proof upon demand of where they acquired the product and if they are pawning it they must have valid identification and serial numbers of the product, if any, are noted. Legitimate retailers - both those operating online and as brick and mortar businesses - as well as consumers have a right to this type of protection.

As I am sure you are aware, retail is an extremely competitive environment and the grocery industry is no exception. In spite of that competitiveness, retailers understand that without cooperating with each other and working together on the investigations of boosters and fences we will not be able to effectively combat this problem. Because of the complexity of ORC cases and the many obstacles that stand in the way of investigating fences, especially internet based fences, it is not unusual for ORC investigators from several different retailers to work together to help gather evidence for law enforcement so that a fence can be shut down.

In spite of Safeway's best efforts and unprecedented alliances with other retailers to combat ORC, we continue to suffer significant losses. If we are to be successful in curtailing this enormous criminal enterprise that threatens the businesses of retailers across the country, costs millions of dollars in lost sales tax revenue and impacts consumers through adulterated product, higher prices and lack of availability of merchandise, we must have strong federal legislation that more clearly defines ORC and requires the same level of accountability on internet sellers as that of traditional retail sites.

I thank you very much for your attention and I look forward to answering any questions you may have.

In: Organized Retail Crime
Editors: Blake H. Liventin
ISBN: 978-1-61122-768-0

Chapter 9

TESTIMONY OF DETECTIVE DAVID HILL, OF THE MONTGOMERY COUNTY, MARYLAND POLICE DEPARTMENT ON BEHALF OF LAW ENFORCEMENT, BEFORE THE SUBCOMMITTEE ON CRIME, TERRORISM AND HOMELAND SECURITY, HEARING ON "ORGANIZED RETAIL THEFT: FOSTERING A COMPREHENSIVE PUBLIC-PRIVATE RESPONSE"

Good Morning Chairman Scott and Ranking Member Forbes, my name is Detective David Hill and I am pleased to be testifying before the subcommittee today on the growing problem of organized retail crime.

By way of background, I am currently a detective with the Montgomery County Police Department's Retail Crimes Unit and have been in law enforcement for over 16 years. I am a sworn Deputy of the U.S. Marshall Service and assigned to the Metro Area Fraud Task Force of the United States Secret Service. I am the *only* detective in my department and one of the few in the region assigned exclusively to investigate retail theft and fraud.

To put my job in perspective, industry-wide retail fraud and theft losses amount to almost $40 billion a year according to one prominent study. That is more than *double* the losses of robbery, burglary, larceny, and auto theft *combined* ($16.9 billion) nationwide. As you know, the Washington Metropolitan Area is the eighth largest in the nation, with thousands of retail outlets and several major malls just in Montgomery County alone. I am a busy man. I typically handle scores of cases each year.

As we have heard, organized retail crime is a real and growing trend, and accounts for a large portion of overall retail losses. According to the National Retail Federation, 79 percent of retailers surveyed report being victims of ORC and 71 percent saw increases in ORC activity last year. The term "organized" can mean many things, from pairs of "boosters" who target retail stores with the intention of distracting a sales associate while the other sweeps merchandise from the shelf, to teams of five or more who stake out targets carefully and steal discreetly in crowded stores. In many cases, ORC teams are efficiently segmented into collectors, packers, and movers that take the stolen merchandise to a waiting car, and still others who serve as lookouts to make sure that the team is not being followed by security.

Some of the more sophisticated criminals engage in changing the UPC bar codes on merchandise so they ring up differently at check-out, this is commonly called "ticket switching." Others use stolen or cloned credit cards to obtain merchandise. Sophisticated or not, what all of these thieves have in common is that they are *career* criminals usually hired by bulk buyers or ring-leaders with specific products in mind. They have "shopping lists," if you will. Some target luxury clothing, accessories, and perfume while others focus on baby formula and expensive over-the-counter medications or beauty aids. Gift cards and electronics are other popular targets. Believe it or not, these criminals are even stealing vacuum cleaners and power tools. Whatever is new; whatever is hot, that's what the criminals want.

Some of these ORC groups travel important interstate corridors, like I-95, from Miami to Maine, hitting numerous retailers along the way and filling vans or trucks with stolen merchandise. In one case, we recovered $40,000 in merchandise that was stolen in one hour. The booty ends up at underground bodegas, pawn shops and flea markets, some is repackaged and warehoused for re-distribution, and, in a growing trend, more and more of it is showing up for sale on the Internet.

The reason so-called "eFencing" is becoming so popular is the simple economics of risk and reward. A typical fencing operation typically pays criminals $.30 cents on the dollar, whereas online marketplaces and auction sites can bring closer to $.70 cents on the dollar for "new in box (NIB)" merchandise, and gift cards pay even more. Further, local pawnshops tend to be regulated – requiring the disclosure of information about both sellers and the merchandise being sold – which creates additional risks for criminals. In contrast, Online marketplaces provide an unregulated environment in which thieves can re-sell stolen property to customers on an national or even international level with few or no questions asked.

The Internet not only makes it easier for ORC rings to unload merchandise at near retail prices, it also enables sophisticated single-operators to realize a huge profit off of their crimes as well. On Christmas Eve 2005 the Montgomery County PD apprehended a college student who was the subject of a CNBC piece on eFencing earlier this year. By his own admission, the student made over $50,000 auctioning off stolen merchandise on e-Bay. These items were stolen from stores such as Best Buy, Target, and Wal-Mart and included high-end computer graphic cards, GPS navigation units, books, expensive iPod accessories, and many other items.

Mr. Chairman, important investigations like this one rely upon the ongoing partnership between law enforcement and the retail sector. While I work a regular investigative beat, cases are most often initiated and reported by the loss prevention investigators employed by retail companies. It is true that many companies like e-Bay will provide information to law enforcement when asked to do so, however, requiring Online auction sites to collect and disclose serial numbers of products being offered for sale when appropriate, and to provide additional seller information to retailers' loss prevention investigators will help our retail partners better understand and build cases that can then be turned over to detectives like myself.

Additionally, as noted above, increased seller disclosures should discourage criminals from even attempting eFencing. Such transparency will likely disproportionately affect and deter criminals who are interested in fencing stolen product Online, with little or no impact on legitimate sellers.

Mr Chairman, I commend the important work that you are doing to shed light on the very real problem of organized retail crime. Too often professional thieves are getting off with little more than a slap on the wrist because many jurisdictions are still treating ORC crimes as shoplifting cases. Some would say that this is a "victimless" crime, but ORC affects society because it increases prices and can compromise the quality and safety of consumer goods. As I have already described, these are often multi-jurisdictional crimes where professional thieves are regularly crossing state lines. With the added component of eFencing on the Internet, this is a natural area for Congress to get involved. Clearly, federal legislation would serve as a powerful tool for law enforcement and a deterrent to would-be criminals.

Mr. Chairman, I appreciate the invitation to address you and the subcommittee members. I welcome any questions or comments you may have.

Thank you.

Chapter Sources

The following chapters have been previously published:

Chapter 1 – This is an edited, excerpted and augmented edition of a United States Congressional Research Service publication, Report Order Code R41118, dated June 16, 2010.

Chapter 2 – These remarks were delivered as Statement of David Johnson, before the United States House Judiciary Subcommittee on Crime, Terrorism, and Homeland Security, dated November 5, 2009.

Chapter 3 – These remarks were delivered as Statement of Janice Ayala, before the United States House Judiciary Subcommittee on Crime, Terrorism, and Homeland Security, dated November 5, 2009.

Chapter 4 – These remarks were delivered as Statement of John R. Large, before the United States House Judiciary Subcommittee on Crime, Terrorism, and Homeland Security, dated November 5, 2009.

Chapter 5 – These remarks were delivered as Statement of Zane M. Hill, before the United States House Judiciary Subcommittee on Crime, Terrorism, and Homeland Security, dated November 5, 2009.

Chapter 6 – These remarks were delivered as Statement of Brad Brekke, before the United States House Judiciary Subcommittee on Crime, Terrorism, and Homeland Security, dated October 25, 2007.

Chapter 7 – These remarks were delivered as Statement of Robert Chesnut, before the United States House Judiciary Subcommittee on Crime, Terrorism, and Homeland Security, dated October 25, 2007.

Chapter 8 – These remarks were delivered as Statement of Karl Langhorst, before the United States House Judiciary Subcommittee on Crime, Terrorism, and Homeland Security, dated October 25, 2007.

Chapter 9 – These remarks were delivered as Statement of Detective David Hill, before the United States House Judiciary Subcommittee on Crime, Terrorism, and Homeland Security, dated October 25, 2007.

INDEX

D

E

S

T

U

V

W

Y